Leigh Welles'
BALLET BODY BOOK

Leigh Welles' BALLET BODY BOOK

Exercises to Reshape Your Body—and Free Your Spirit

by Leigh Welles

Edited by Jessica Deutsch

THE BOBBS-MERRILL COMPANY, INC.
Indianapolis / New York

Published by The Bobbs-Merrill Co., Inc.
Indianapolis/New York
Manufactured in the United States of America
First Printing
Designed by Barbara Hall
Illustrations by Thea Kliros

**Library of Congress Cataloging in Publication
Data**

Welles, Leigh.
  Leigh Welles' Ballet body book.

  1. Ballet dancing. I. Title. II. Title:
Ballet body book.
GV1788.W44 792.8′2 82-4202
ISBN 0-672-52701-4   AACR2

To my children, Eric and Hope,
for their loving encouragement, support,
and strength of character

Contents

Leigh Welles'
BALLET BODY BOOK

△ Symbol of Change

Think of life as a triangle bound by earth, water, and sky. Can you travel around the triangle's points to make your life complete, fulfilled?

The triangle represents, for me, the wholeness of a human being. We start in an earthbound corner and then must move across the waters of our life: the periods of change and fluctuating circumstance. Finally we move upward—there are no shortcuts—toward the sky: the pinnacle of our achievements, the fulfillment of our potential.

Used symbolically in astronomy, mythology, and religion, an equilateral triangle is a symbol of the trinity. It is the structure on which my own experience is based.

PART I

PART 1

△ Changing the Course of a Life

There was never a moment, as far back in my life as I can remember, when I did not know what I wanted to do: I had to express what I felt through music. And I wanted the world to see, to feel, and to be as touched as I was by the beauty and truth in music.

I wanted to dance; I *had* to dance. And I was lucky enough to become a pupil of Victoria Sheffield Cassan, Anna Pavlova's disciple and friend, who was all I wanted some day to be. Cassan told me that I danced as though I had a song in my heart, and that was indeed the way I felt.

At the age of eighteen I went to England, where I joined the Original Ballet Russe as a soloist. I

should have been ecstatic, but I was often misera-
ble. The company's devotion to art and beauty
was tainted by the petty jealousies and competition that existed among the dancers. The company's artistic difficulties were eventually
submerged by financial ones, and the company
was finally disbanded in London.

At this point, one of my dearest teachers, Lydia
Sokolova, who had danced with the Ballet Russe
under Diaghilev, encouraged me to go to Paris and
audition for a major company while it was there.
On the morning of the audition I reread the wonderful recommendation she had written for me
and walked confidently out into the street, certain
that I would be chosen.

Suddenly I was aware of all the people bustling
around me, so absorbed in their own lives. I
thought of the dancers in the company I had just
left. The world of art was really no different from
the world outside. In both there was a preoccupa-
tion with self. Who among them all cared about
glorifying truth or touching hearts? *Everybody*
seemed to be competing, suspicious, looking only
to his or her own survival.

What if the new company were no different?
What if, in the face of the same disillusionment I
had experienced with the Ballet Russe, I lost my
faith in the beauty and truth I had been taught to
transmit? What if I were not strong enough to sus-

tain the concepts passed down to me from Anna Pavlova? I could not bear to lose that vision of the spirit I had grown up wishing to serve. I stopped in the street, afraid—and I turned back.

At that moment, I changed the course of my life. My naïveté, my inability to balance a dream against reality made me retreat to my earthbound corner. Without knowing it, I had begun the descent down the side of my "triangle" to the bottom of my life. It took twenty years for me to reach it.

Upon my return to America, I put the artistic part of my life into a deep freeze. Marriage seemed to me to be a happy alternative. But the early years of marriage were disappointing. My husband had promised that we would move to New York; instead, he found countless excuses to remain in the Midwest. I missed the cultural excitement of the city and felt isolated. Beginning to despair, I took my frustration to the church and was told that a marriage should be saved at all costs.

Motherhood seemed to be the next compensation for having sacrificed my life as a dancer. We had a boy, then a girl. I loved both children, but it bothered me that I did not feel as though "mother" was my role in life. Perhaps *looking* matronly would help me *feel* matronly—so I cut my long hair and stopped caring about my figure, stopped caring about style. My mind turned as flabby as my body.

Retreating still further into a corner, I shut music out of my life. Where it once had made me soar, it was now making me cry.

I became a devout church member, hoping to find an expression of truth and beauty there. But I discovered that that organization was more interested in the outward form of being a Christian than in the expression of compassionate love itself.

We bought a house, but it soon felt like a prison.

One night, at three o'clock in the morning, actually, I reached a turning point. Both children had been experiencing one illness after the other. I was exhausted from sleepless nights and prayed for inspiration. Hoping to make them feel better, I left my bed, threw a blanket over the dining-room table, and put a small lamp under it. I took the children from their beds and told them we were going to play "house." If only I could break the *atmosphere* of a troubled home, I felt, healing could begin. I made popcorn and took it into our little "house." I acted as if they were healthy, and they responded. That scene of acting "as if" carried *me* along as well. I felt suddenly soothed and happy participating in this spontaneity. We were all responding to the power of joy! My ever-deepening appreciation for the spirit of childlikeness began right then.

Our children grew and went to school. I felt alone again, but the quality of simple joy they had reawakened was still there inside me, seeking to be recaptured elsewhere. I tried cooking lessons and tennis, but trying to "fit in" only made me feel more left out. And I got no support from my husband, who convinced me that I was an unloving woman.

Still looking for some kind of creative purpose to my life, I took an evening job teaching classes in ballroom dancing at a private school. How on earth, I wondered, had all my training come to this? The money I earned, however, helped me set up a small ballet school in the basement of our house. This was "permissible" since it didn't take me away from home. Local children came for lessons, along with a couple of out-of-shape women who wanted exercise. I often thought they might be saying, "How can she be any good if she has to teach in her basement!"

One day a severely retarded child of eighteen, an overweight, ungainly girl who was an epileptic, was brought to me by her grandmother. The girl was about to be institutionalized, and her grandmother asked me to take care of her, to give her a chance for the better life she deserved.

After seemingly endless days and nights of hard work with the girl, I was utterly weary. I prayed to God to know why I, who loved beauty so much, should be dealing with grossness. The answer seemed to be that only with a firm vision of real beauty could one cope with distortion. I learned to hold in my mind a picture of this child as normal, regardless of the outer picture she presented. At the same time, I had to allow my imagination to think and feel as she did so that I could understand and reach her. This two-way stretch between the perfect and the imperfect showed me how to hold the mental image of that which is good and beautiful while I dealt with that which was wrong and ugly. While maintaining a better image of my pupil, I demanded that she conform to the conduct, habits, and attitudes that would be consistent with that better image. And so she gradually learned to control her moods, her appetite, and even most of her epileptic seizures. She learned to complete tasks, to read simple books for enjoyment, even to go to the store by herself. In three years she went from being unkempt, disagreeable, and uncontrollable to an attractive, happy, twenty-one-year-old girl who wore a size eight dress. Together, we overcame many of the limitations that had been laid down by doctors and members of her family.

I turned forty and wondered where I had gone wrong. How had I lost the passion for life I had once had? I had to find out if there was any life left for me. And so I took a trip to New York—back to that center of the arts. There the vitality and freedom of the city taught me I still had inner reserves of beauty and strength and that they had value. I discovered I was not cold and unresponsive—I was passionate and alive.

Grappling with what I was coming to regard as brainwashing by my husband, I forced myself to examine every aspect of our relationship. I found an entirely different picture from the one I had believed before. Facing the truth at last, I needed a way to handle the traps that had held me. I knew the secret lay in the technique I had used on my retarded pupil. Now I had to practice this method on myself. I had to see the truth: I had to confront the reality of the man to whom I was married. When I looked at my circumstances with candor, I saw all that I had pushed "under the rug." My mind reeled, but I knew I had to escape.

One afternoon my son, sensing my great distress, asked me to listen to his latest record. We turned the stereo up as loud as it would go, and he and my daughter and I danced and sang at the tops of our voices. At that moment I made the conscious decision to allow music to come back into my life. I would respond again, I knew, to the spirit of freedom and energy and joy that music and life held. I would use music to lift me out of my earthbound corner. I held up a fresh vision for myself. In time, this vision took me out of that house to a new life and a new realization of myself. This time I did not turn back.

I am not the only woman who has ever felt trapped. This book speaks for all women, at whatever age, who have experienced some of the feelings I have described. It is never too late to face the reality of your own world. You are never too old to do something about it.

△ Facing Reality: It's Never Too Late

Look in the mirror. You may think you see yourself, but you're wrong—you are seeing only an image. You may be trapped beneath that image. My aim is to release the inner you and, in so doing, to *change* the reflection in the mirror.

I did it. It is true that my strict classical training as a dancer taught me how to be strong, both mentally and physically, but I had allowed that strength to be submerged. At forty-two I made a new beginning toward happiness and the realization of myself. You too can begin again.

I have taken the techniques of discipline and freedom of spirit imbued in me by ballet and turned them into a program and a way of life. If you follow my method, you, too, will not only look marvelous—you will feel better than you have ever felt before.

There have been scores of exercise books written for women, with careful diagrams of kicks and bends designed to flatten flabby stomachs and trim heavy thighs. I've seen women pounce upon these books sure that, at last, *this* one will work for them. Within a month these women are back stalking the bookstores, in search of yet another exercise or diet book.

I am not offering new "tricks." My book is not something you pick up for ten minutes each morning to rid your conscience of your daily obligation to firm weak muscles. These pages include a way of *thinking* that will show you how to teach and sustain yourself; to make the most of yourself.

It takes courage to do this. It requires faith, patience, and persistence. You may think you don't have the discipline to build both a better you and a better life, but we all have the power within ourselves.

I've heard all the excuses there are for ignoring the body and the self: "I have no time . . . too tired . . . too busy with children . . . too many demands . . . not enough money . . . too vain." I have heard one particular excuse from almost *every* woman over thirty: "It's too late for me," or, "I'm too old."

These are the recognizable fences we put around ourselves, but what about the other restrictions we impose? Here lies the challenge. How many of you are scared to look at your own hidden potential? At the delightful, graceful spirit you may have buried or crushed years ago? Has the inner you been sacrificed to a husband and children or to the demands of a career?

Why do we allow ourselves to be limited to the stereotyped roles of "intellectual" business woman, "manicured" secretary, "dowdy" spinster, "harassed" housewife, or "bored" socialite?

Why don't such women explore their *full* identities, their *real* individualities? Who says they have to be molded so rigidly? The new woman of our time has crossed many barriers and is learning to master more than one job. If modern attitudes about careers and life-styles can change, why shouldn't there be a new way of looking at our inner beings? We can ask for and expect more. The spirit of the whole woman, which lies within all of us, can be released.

This spirit, which is the fundamental principle of my teaching, is the vital essence of all of us. I see it as the wholeness of one's self and the world around that self. It is spiritual energy that courses through every animated being like an electric current. We can plug into this invisible but powerful current of life. If you are denying this force, this part of yourself, then you are depressed, bogged down, empty and stale, and your body reflects the way you feel.

I don't care where you are right now—how young or how old you are. I believe that you can release a potential you never dreamed was possible. Until now you have let a thousand self-imposed concepts and external circumstances prevent this from happening. Challenge those old arguments of limitation, guilt, and self-denial. Take time out for yourself. Whatever you spend now on your physical and mental well-being can prevent doctors' bills later.

In this book I'm talking about real change. I don't believe in slapping a veneer on top of what's troublesome. The change I mean starts from the inside. First, you must understand yourself; then you can proceed to change.

Remember, no one but you can bring about this change. Change can be the hardest thing for anyone to accomplish. Too often we would rather stay in old houses, old love affairs, old self-images rather than fight and take responsibility for our lives. What is familiar is too often equated with right. To change means to be uncomfortable until practice turns the new way into the natural way. It is not easy. Start, for now, by accepting from me the glimmer of an idea that you might be able to do something about yourself and your life. This first acceptance—this giving permission to yourself to succeed—is the most difficult part of the evolution. It is scary, for a hundred things will seem to fight against it. But once you can assimilate into your being the concept of a changing and progressing you, you are halfway there. My techniques are designed to help you fight to achieve your right to this new idea of yourself and then to keep it.

When I finally forced myself to realize I did not want the life I was living, I knew I had to let go of the past. I had to find strength somewhere. I gave myself a command to find that strength within me: to grow up and not depend on others. This was the beginning of what became my new mental and physical strength. I fought the flabby mental muscles that had helped imprison me. If there was a technique that worked for the body, there must be one that would strengthen the mind as well. I had to practice replacing thoughts of self-doubt, anxiety, and guilt with affirmations of faith in myself and my future. As the body responds to discipline so did my mind.

I am no psychoanalyst. I speak of what I know from personal experience and from what I have observed in the many, many women I have taught. I have seen the results of taking control of your life and your mind.

If you're in your twenties, you can use this book

to free your potential now by learning to put to work those inner forces that will shape your mind and your body into a happy and beautiful "self" for life.

If you're in your thirties, you can use these techniques to help nourish the body and soul of someone who has most likely already given years of her life to a husband and children. I will help you rediscover your identity and bring back your energy—as well as the flat stomach you once had. If you are midway in your career, exhausted by the efforts of competing, I will teach you how to restore your vitality, how to release the tension you feel in your shoulders and neck.

For those of you who are resigned to seeing your forties as middle age—don't be resigned. Youthful beauty and energy can be yours by learning how to tap the wisdom and experience of your years. You'll find your new "self" entering the most productive and fulfilling time of your life.

If you are in your fifties or beyond, I offer you a challenge to join me in tearing down the old barrier of age limitations. Let's see how far we can go together; the future is full of promise, and it's going to be fun.

Wherever you are in the passage of your life, this book is for you. I know how it feels to be tired, to be out of shape, overweight, feeling old and "used up." I'm here to tell you that you *do* have another chance—a chance to feel younger, stronger, healthier, and more beautiful than you have ever felt before.

We are no different, you and I. I did it. So can you.

Fundamentals of
△ the Leigh Welles
Method

The Leigh Welles method is a new concept of exercise that starts from the inside rather than the outside. It builds on an art form rather than on athleticism. It is not dull, repetitive or gymnastic. It is based on simplified ballet techniques and aesthetic principles. From these movements and concepts, I have developed a class that proves effective for women of all ages.

Now don't shudder and tell me that you hate your body; that you're too clumsy, badly proportioned, or too old. I am not concerned now with your shape or the way you move or how much flesh is hidden beneath your clothing. What we'll start with is you as a person with feelings, attitudes, and desires. You must work with those feelings first, as we do in ballet. I want you to learn to identify and respond to your spirit, to encourage that spirit toward beauty and ease. Only then will your body relax and move correctly.

You know the inspiration you feel when you hear music or are enraptured by the dance? It is the giving up of the "self" to the universality of art, identifying one's own inner rhythm with the external rhythm of life. Everything in the universe has this rhythm. We make the most progress when we learn how to work with it, not against it.

Sadly, we have lost touch with this spiritual flow because we allow the speed and pressures of our daily lives to crowd it out. To be in contact with it, to be at one with it, means to feel inner harmony and external control—and what good things these are to feel!

My method, based as it is on ballet, is concerned as much with this "spirit" as it is the body. It feeds your inner need for beauty while providing you with the instruction to express it physically. While strengthening your body, you will rediscover grace, spontaneity, and poise. I promise you a freeing up of yourself. Keeping in touch with your inner spirit, yielding to it, produces your own real beauty—beauty that transcends the superficial prettiness of the model or the movie star.

I admire the woman of our times who has stepped into her rightful place as the equal of men in business and the professions. I also applaud the woman who has achieved equal recognition in the arts and sciences. But let's not be afraid to feel more beautiful! Let's combine that feeling with gentle strength and imaginative use of our talents, and let's try to like ourselves at the same time that we are trying so hard to make the rest of the world like us.

It takes courage to be beautiful, especially for intelligent and creative women. Even today, a beautiful woman is not always taken seriously but is looked upon as a sex object or a piece of decoration. Women must first challenge this image in themselves. Why should our choice be limited to "intimidated femininity" or "tough broad"? Start now to reshape your body to serve a lovelier and freer spirit. Start now to take hold of this concept of a deeper beauty.

The Leigh Welles method will do for you what it does for the ballerina. It will reshape you, redefine you, strengthen you. You must start to view your body as a piece of sculpture. You must chisel away at the layers encasing the beauty beneath your exterior self. You will uncover the symmetry and the naturally lovely lines you have and don't yet see. In following my method, you become both the work of art *and* the artist.

I know my method works because I have tested it on myself. In my late thirties my body was miserably out of shape. I tried all kinds of exercise but each was incomplete. In fact, my condition deteriorated because, as I began to focus on it, I became increasingly disgusted with it and with myself. And so, hating myself, I abused my body by stuffing it with food, and that in turn dulled my mind with self-condemnation.

Finally, I realized that I had been searching everywhere for something I'd had all along—my own ballet training. Could I go through that kind of rigorous training again? No. But I *could* simplify and adapt it and make use of what ballet had taught me—discipline, feeling, and mental strength. As I unravelled the part of myself that had been submerged in the years of marriage, my depression began to lift, and, like a forgotten violin being retuned, my body responded to the frustrated artist in me. That is how the Leigh Welles method was born.

You are not a machine to be revved up with a quick exercise routine and then put aside. You are the most marvelously integrated instrument on earth. See yourself in this way. You must not be afraid to learn how and what to play on this instrument of beauty. I don't care how many obstacles you see between where you are and what I am telling you you are capable of feeling and doing. I have been able to communicate the spirit of artistic work and positive change to women in my classes who have made of my method something that extends beyond the hour spent in the studio. It is my hope that this book will help you to experience this as well.

Since the way to your body is through your mind and soul, you must put yourself into the correct mental framework for this creative and corrective process. Your positive attitude toward this concept is essential for your success.

Ballet is the language of the body, but remember—it is a *language*. It is a creative expression, a turning outward from within. If a dancer trains herself to use this language, she is in touch with her deepest feelings. She is able to discipline her body through keen self-awareness, and that disciplined body provides her, in turn, with the instrument to express her emotive energies.

Goethe said: "Whatever you can do, or dream you can, begin it./There is boldness, genius, power, and magic in it."

Don't be scared away by whatever the word "ballet" conjures up in your imagination. You don't have to wear a tutu and prance about on pointe shoes, but you do have to learn what it means to discipline your body.

Ballet will, in time, change your mental concept

of yourself. If you were now to draw yourself as you would like to be, you'd probably sketch a flat-stomached, slim-thighed, sylphlike creature, but I wonder if you would question how this sylph thought or felt? I wonder if, in the rushed hours of your day, as you devote yourself to children, home, business deals, and work, you ever think such a thing. Feeling! We have all been taught to externalize ourselves so much that this word has almost lost meaning for us, and yet it is feeling that directs one's spirit and character.

Begin to paint a new picture of yourself upon the canvas of your life. Create a mental image of the *person* you aspire to be—not just the body—a *person* with thoughts, feelings, and passion. Keep this image in your mind as, with the principles of this book, you work toward a changed body.

How does my program differ from other exercises? Tennis and jogging, both immensely popular with women today, produce nothing like the effects on the body that ballet exercises do. For feminine beauty you cannot compare the legs of a runner with the smooth, tapered ones of a dancer. Only ballet exercise lifts weight out of the hips and thighs. Tennis cannot slenderize the inner thighs or firm the upper arms. It cannot control a spreading seat.

All competitive sports have some negative effect on the body. For most, the strain and tension of competition cause the body to tense rather than to relax and be free. The set, determined jaw of the female competitor reflects pressure that the ballet-exercised woman learns to release. Ballet brings out the potential of a woman's own sleek bodily grace.

The secrets of body shaping and control lie in the techniques of Russian classical ballet. Today, all forms of athletics are beginning to acknowledge and to seek this underlying body discipline. In a study conducted by the Institute of Sports Medicine and Trauma at the Lenox Hill Hospital in New York, ballet ranked as the most demanding physical activity—ahead of basketball, soccer, and football. How else does a Baryshnikov achieve such control and elevation with his leaps and jumps?

Most aerobic exercises foster the notion that the more kicks and movements the body executes, the more that body will accomplish. Nothing could be further from the truth. What if there is little or no attention paid to the spine? When the spine is allowed to "sink" into the hips and abdomen while kicking, the body's strength is being torn down, not built up. Thighs and buttocks will gradually get bigger from this downward pressure. The kick that ballet teaches slims the thighs. The reason for this is that ballet calls for the seat to be tight, the buttocks and hips lifted, and the spine straight as a prerequisite to the kick.

If the muscles in the back are weak and the vertebrae sag, you endanger the parts of the body above and below. The muscles of the stomach soften, and the internal organs of the body weaken. Additionally, the knees of the average adult are not prepared for the continual "hammering" of too much jogging or jumping.

Women's exercise needs are very different from men's. Everything in my training successfully challenges the downward gravity that time and age exert on women's breasts (sagging), stomach (protruding), buttocks (falling), and thighs (spreading).

In indiscriminate exercising or jogging, most women allow the weight of their bodies to fall, that is, they press down, over and over again, into those very areas they ought to be pulling in and pulling up.

Even the relatively few athletically strong women who can keep their entire torsos' weight out of their hips and off their legs still pay the price of heavily muscle-bound legs. The legs of the correctly trained ballet dancer, who probably exercises more often and more rigorously, remain shapely and sleek. Every serious jogger who has come to my school has had tight calf muscles and found it hard to stretch her entire body. Muscles that are exercised and strong are valuable, but they are more graceful if they are also relaxed, limber, and supple in movement.

From the Mental Framework to the Basics of the Body

With my method, you must work from the inside out—starting with the very skeleton of your body.

THE SPINE

The most essential component of a strong and healthy body is the spine, the vertebrae of which can be compared to the floors of a building. The spine is the internal support meant to keep each floor (or vertebra) of your body separate from the others. A straight spine is the first essential of my method.

I often see women "sitting" back on their heels and sinking into their hips. In so doing, they throw their spines off balance, which can cause backache, stomach pains and even headaches.

The small of the back, the lowest five vertebrae, is often the problem area that results from bad posture. To achieve a straight spine, you are going to have to pull that lower section of your back upward—lifting and thus straightening it.

The spine is designed to have each bone separated by a cushion of space, and muscles in your back are meant to carry out that task. But as you went through life carrying heavy books to school, then groceries home, and then bore babies, you began "sinking" into your abdomen, letting your weight rest on your hips. If you carry that bad habit into your thirties and forties, you will be the classic candidate for backache, protruding stomach, and heavy thighs and hips.

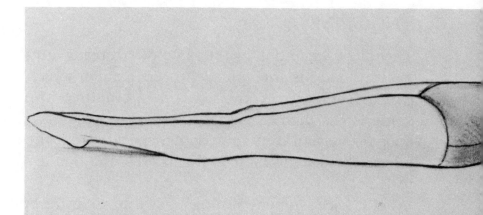

Exercise 1

Try this. Lie down on the floor. Stretch your arms over your head as far back as they will go. Grasp one wrist and, remaining flat on the floor, pull through the entire length of the body in opposite directions. Hold that pull, stretching your legs flat, knees straight and together, and—take note—point your toes as hard as possible. Now pull your tummy in and up, toward your hands. Finally, press your lower spine down into the floor. Remember, there are four distinct steps: pull arms; stretch legs to pointed toes; suck stomach in and up; flatten spine to floor.

Take the time, now, to try this exercise. It calls for concentration to do all four steps simultaneously. Test yourself. Move out of your reading mind and into your performing body.

If you have now tried this exercise, you will have felt the substantial exertion required. You will also have felt an immediate stretch and straightening effect on your spine. Now, stand up as you normally do and try the same thing. You can't? Of course not. When you were lying down, the floor provided the support. When you stand up, *you* have to provide it—and your back muscles are not yet strong enough.

Muscles *can* regain their strength, however, no matter what your age. I began to rebuild mine at forty. As you learn to practice my exercises, those back muscles will get stronger until they are able to lift all those vertebrae and straighten your spine.

THE UPPER LEGS

Do you have an accumulation of soft fat on your thighs and seat? There is no magic cure for this, but there *is* a remedy. With the right exercises, legs can become thinner, firmer, and smoother; the buttocks smaller and tighter.

Fat is lost when it is broken up and stretched. As fat is displaced, it sometimes softens before it goes away. So, for a smoother, thinner, firmer leg, you must know how to control the fat and muscles. "Stretch" means moving in two directions. You stretch (and thereby lose fat) by pulling your weight up and off your hips, by taking the pressure off your legs and out of your seat. To do this, you need a strong spine. Once you can lift the weight of your body from the supporting leg, you can execute a correct kick.

And so we are brought back to the spine. The spine alone provides real support. Without a strong back, all the kicking in the world will not help. If you are "sitting" on the fat each time you kick, you are only pushing your weight farther down and, like a lump of dough, it spreads. Only by inwardly pulling your weight up, taking pressure off the thighs, will you have the action that slims and shapes.

Exercise 2

Stand in front of a mirror with your legs uncovered. Straighten your spine. Put your feet together. Watch what happens to your legs when you "pull up" the fat over your kneecaps.

Now, see if you can go one step further and use the thigh muscles to literally change the contour of the upper legs by lifting and rotating the muscles of the upper thighs outward and *up*. Keep the inside of your thighs pressed together and your seat tight. When your muscles are strong enough to do this, you will be able to see the fat lift, stretch, and appear taut or smooth.

Don't be discouraged if you are not able to achieve this right away. It often takes weeks or months of practicing these exercises correctly for the thighs to respond to your demand. You must keep the mental image of that finished form before you. Lose your inner vision and you lose your chance of success. You're not just training your back and leg muscles. You're practicing faith in the potential of your new body.

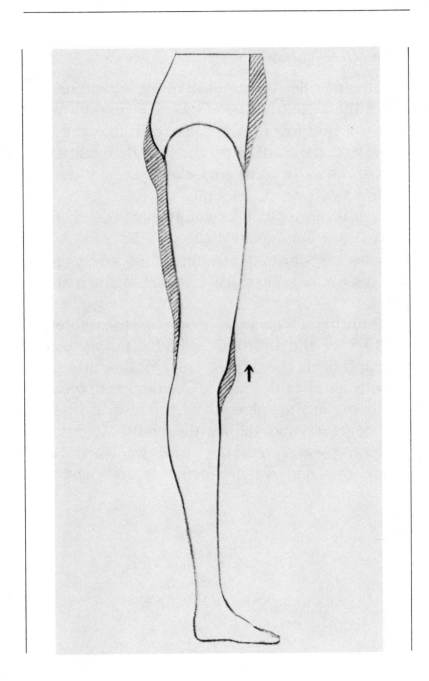

THE BUTTOCKS

Nothing handles the problem of the spreading seat better than the training of ballet technique. Why? Because nothing provides exercise like the plié, the relevé, the battement, the port de bras, which over and over train the muscles to strengthen and control this part of the body.

No, it is not too late for you to start that training even if you are overweight and in your fifties! Muscles respond to conditioning at any age—fat reduces under an exercise and diet regimen at any point.

All during my classes we practice the tightening together of the buttocks, which diminishes the seat and firms the thighs. This "pulling together" of both sides of the buttocks, combined with the stretching of the spine out of the hips, draws the seat together and refines the body. We practice "gripping" and relaxing until we learn to be aware of when we are doing it and when we aren't!

Exercise 3

Try this yourself. Stand with your feet together and pinch your seat together as tightly as you can. Hold it for a few seconds and relax. Everytime you are waiting for a bus, or standing in line, practice this and you will begin to feel and see a difference if you combine it with these other exercises.

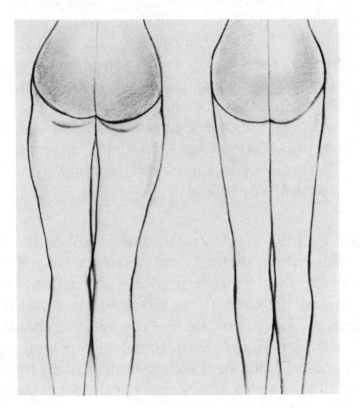

THE ARMS

In any truly feminine body, the soft curve of the arms conveys both grace and elegance. Gracefulness is not a gift. With practice, you can achieve it.

Exercise 4

Make a circle with your arms in front of you, below your breasts, as though you're holding a beach ball. Separate your hands by approximately 12 inches. Stretch the fingers, as if to meet the corresponding fingers of the opposite hand. Try to lift the elbows toward the ceiling. Keep the shoulders down. Now drop the left arm. Roll the right wrist slightly open. You are now in the correct position for a graceful handshake.

Did that feel too artificial and affected? As though it belonged to another age? You may indeed feel awkward until practice produces strength in your arms and the effort in the exercise eases you into a natural movement. Believe me, natural shoulder grace is very much appreciated in our own age. You should cultivate a feeling of depth and roundness to your torso. Every move of the arms should

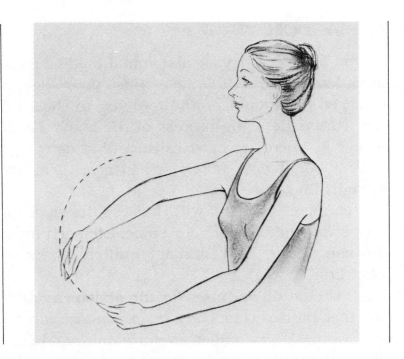

begin at the center of your back—not at the hand or elbow.

When you're sitting, let your arms rest softly in your lap while your spine stays straight. Shoulders should be loose and relaxed, as though falling away from the straight spine. The elbows hang loosely away from the body, leaving a feeling of air and space. Hugging your elbows to your body only makes you look awkward, cold, or scared. To complete this graceful appearance, sit slightly forward, at a slight angle to your chair, ankles crossed, spine erect.

THE ABDOMEN

Do you believe that your abdominal holding muscles deteriorate with age? Has your doctor shrugged his shoulders and told you to cheer up and accept the aging process of the body? Don't believe it. There are muscles there that don't "go away," but it does take work to give them the strength they once had.

Once more, we start with basics—the small of your back, the base of your spine. Stomach muscles can't grab, hold, and lift until the back is lifted first.

You should do exercises for the abdomen daily. No other part of your body requires more consistent work. Every ballet exercise in this book, when practiced diligently, serves to strengthen the stomach muscles. No one exercise can help you entirely on its own. They must be practiced together because the overall strength of your body is necessary in order for the abdomen to pull itself in and up—and, once up, to stay there.

When your abdomen is lifted and holding its own, your waistline will then also have a chance to come up out of your hips and become slim.

Exercise 5

Stand up and stretch your spine. Now, contract your stomach muscles and simultaneously pull in and lift up the inside of your body. Hold 3 counts without letting go. Make a further effort to contract deeper inside. Hold for 3 more counts and relax. Repeat several times.

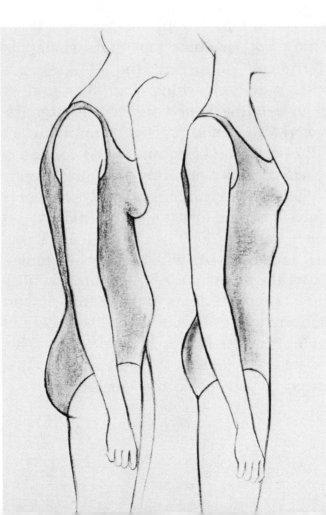

> Remember what it's like to drink with a straw, trying to get the last dregs from the bottom of the glass? Now, see if you can reach down inside yourself and draw yourself up as you would a sip of water. Pull yourself out of your hips. Don't raise your shoulders. This is the way your stomach must learn to feel at all times.

In the beginning, if your muscles are very soft, you may not feel that too much is happening. Keep trying. Contracting and pulling up those muscles is like clenching your fists and at the same time lifting your hands. This exercise will take work. You must practice it until you experience the sensation of tightness and control. It can be practiced any place, any time. I often practice this when I ride elevators or wait for someone.

In my forties, it took me a long time to get my stomach flat. So don't get impatient. This technique, once learned, will keep your stomach in shape for the rest of your life. Again, visualization of the desired result is helpful and important. Remember, too, that you can help those muscles by giving them a lighter burden to lift. The less you weigh, obviously, the less muscle strength you need in your back and stomach.

Don't let anyone fool you into thinking you can change quickly. It took you a long time to arrive at your body's present condition. It will take time to change it. Anything worth doing is usually done slowly and takes time. Look for monthly changes, not weekly ones.

THE KNEES, ANKLES, AND FEET

Let's move down to the knees, ankles, and feet. How we all take them for granted! If you want to see the long-term results of a careless attitude, take a look at an older woman walking down the street. Would she have the confidence to kneel down and the strength in her knees to get back up? Are her feet rigid—moving like lifeless blocks of wood? It is not necessarily her age that has produced these results but inactivity. Lack of exercise does to body joints what lack of oil does to machinery. Both will "rust" and deteriorate. There is no more valuable exercise for the proper maintenance of the knees and legs than the plié at the ballet barre. There is no better strengthener for the feet and ankles than the relevé. (These are terms I'll explain later.)

I bet you never really thought about the strength in your knees, the flexibility of your feet, the control of your ankles. Well, now it's time to devote some attention to them.

45

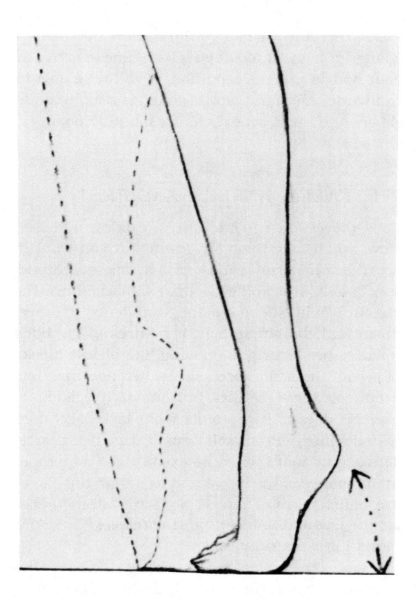

Exercise 6

Try kneeling with one knee on the floor while you hold onto the knob of a closed door. Keep your back straight, your seat underneath you as you rise. Repeat with the other knee on the floor. Do this 4 times.

Now, still holding the door knob, stand up and raise yourself on the balls of both feet, lifting your heels off the floor as far as they will go. Come down gently. Repeat slowly and smoothly 10 times.

Now try "pedaling," first one foot and then the other (in a toe, ball, heel motion) into the floor—rather like running in place in slow motion.

If these exercises make you feel stiff, or if the exercises seem difficult, then you'd better get busy. The joints in your knees need a gentle workout daily, not weekly or monthly. The smooth motion of the ballet plié both oils and conditions these joints and muscles.

I always feel compassion for that little circumference called the ankle. Such a small area expected to do so much. Where would our whole superstructure be without a strong first floor? Relative to the size of the rest of your structure, have you ever seen such a small first floor? Obviously the little muscles of the ankle and foot must be very strong to support everything above. Strengthening the ankles through the correct practice of ballet pliés and relevés will enable you to lift the ankle bones, raise the arch or instep of the foot and thereby provide the correct and strong base for the legs to be straight and the spine to be properly centered.

Your feet and ankles support your whole body. If they are weak, they will throw the whole superstructure out of alignment. I have witnessed many physical problems that vanished when the feet and ankles were strengthened and held correctly.

THE FACE AND NECK

People often ask me how I keep my skin and face so young looking. They are absolutely sure that I have had all kinds of secret face lifts or treatments. The truth is that I do very little for my face besides wash it and use a light moisturizing cream. Outside of what I have inherited, I believe my philosophy and attitudes have done more for my skin and face than any complicated "beauty" treatments ever could. Why? Because my treatments work from the inside toward the outside rather than the reverse.

For example, I apply one of the principles of my philosophy to my face. Too many people abuse their faces and cause the skin to wrinkle by allowing their negative, self-pitying feelings to drag down the lines of their expression. Now we all have negative feelings, but it is the way we handle them that makes the difference. I try to overcome them quickly by identifying the unhappy emotion—anger, tension, self-pity, anxiety—and practicing its opposite and positive replacement. It shows immediately on my face. So, by being "upward" in spirit, I keep the muscles of my face going "upward" too.

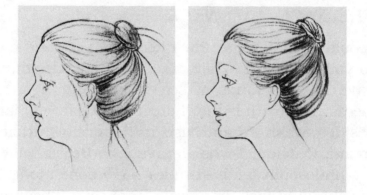

Exercise 7

Stand in front of the mirror. Think and feel tired. Add anxiousness, concern, worry, and any other negative feeling that occurs to you. How does your face look? Now smile. See the difference? Watch what happens to the skin. Smooth your forehead, and don't let those brows knit together. Feel your eyelids and the area around your eyes lift. Let the artist in you go to work. Let your mind conjure up a feeling of joy and enthusiasm so that you feel happy in *spite* of everything. Don't forget that it is just as hard to practice lifting the spirit as it is to lift a leg.

Dare yourself to feel happy, no matter what. Here, too, practice is the key to natural ease.

It always amazes me that a woman can be more concerned about the appearance of her thighs than she is about the expression on her face. The muscles of your face are no different from the muscles in any other part of your body. They have to be trained and disciplined. They have to be taught to "lift," as the rest of your body does. That is why I include the face in this initial set of exercises. You may find, as I have, that by forcing your facial muscles up, you actually influence your feelings to be more positive.

We know that a body in good physical condition helps the skin to be healthy too. When my body returned to an active state, my skin tone and color improved tremendously.

Now for the neck. If you allow the head to hang heavily (to squash and press into the body like the settling of a cushion into a chair), you are going to affect your neck and skin adversely. Instead, while pressing your shoulders down, try to make your neck longer. Stretch upward behind the ears without raising your chin. Try this and see if it doesn't take some of the weight off your neck and, as a result, off its skin. Visualize your neck as long and elegant and your chest as soft, smooth, and uplifted—like a beautiful dove.

THE POSTURE

Let's take an overall look now at the way you stand. Not understanding the spine can give you wrong ideas about posture. The spine should simply be held straight, which permits all the body parts to fit freely and correctly in their normal positions. Shoulders should *not* be pushed back. Seats should *not* be tucked under. Because most women have rounded seats, as opposed to the flat ones of men, the outer contour of the lower portion of your back will appear curved. The business of placing your entire back against a wall to achieve an *externally* straight appearance pushes the seat under and thereby sacrifices the *internal* straightness of the spine. You must train yourself to "see" and feel the straightness of your spine from within.

Exercise 8

Stand up straight with your feet together. Place three-fourths of your entire weight on the balls of your feet with knees relaxed, not rigid. Your breasts should be over your toes, not over your stomach. Don't worry, you won't fall forward. *But it should feel as though you will.* Think about the lowest part of your back and try to elongate it toward the ceiling. Visualize

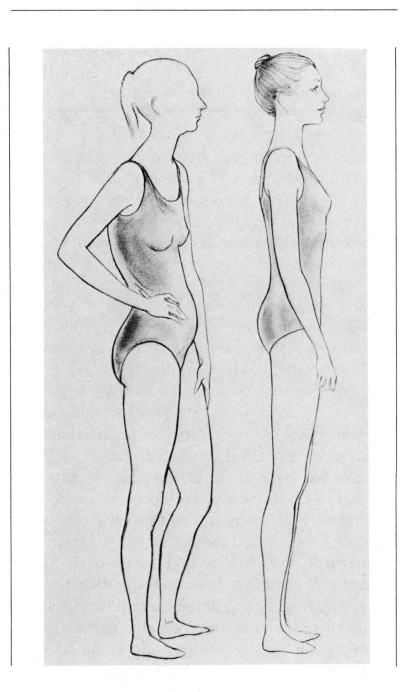

each vertebra being separated by a cushion of air. Try to feel that each bone is under the one on top of it but not resting on it. Continue to visualize the straightness of your spine, which should be neither curved under you nor pushed out behind you. Stretch the upper back (leave your shoulders alone), and lift the ribcage. If you've done this properly, you will be able to feel the *inside* of your stomach lift. Keep the back of your head in line with your spine. By now, you are probably straining your shoulders and "can't breathe." Lower or drop the shoulders naturally, like heavy silk. If your spine is held straight, the shoulders should be placed neither forward *nor* backward, but in the middle of your frame. Try not to drop the rest of the torso with the shoulders. As for breathing, it will take a lot of practice before you will be able to stand this way naturally and breathe easily. Again, I must emphasize that ease comes with practice and consistent work. Now, if most of your body weight is still over the balls of your feet, you are standing correctly. Expect this to feel quite different. It is not easy to change a habit of feeling, but remember, if the way you stand feels the same, you will look the same.

More of other exercises later. However, don't practice them until you've finished reading the book so that they are part of a whole routine. Disjointed exercises that are not fitted into a program can strain rather than train muscles. I have asked you to try the exercises in this chapter just to give you an initial feeling for the parts of your body. But remember that physical feeling is not complete if it is not motivated by the spirit within.

△ Food: How to △ Go into Training

The constant focus on change throughout these pages brings us to the questions of how? why? to what?

For those answers each person must look inside herself. You are reading this book because you want to change. Have you reached the time when you are ready to move out of your corner and let go of the "security" of the world and the mold you have created for yourself, as I did in my fortieth year?

As you accept this challenge, you will encounter frequent and recurring uncertainties. The reserves you must draw upon are basic but difficult in themselves. Take honesty for one. Do you really want to change? Or do you merely want to improve your looks and life while hanging on to the old habits and beliefs that produced those looks and that life? Will you have faith in your strength, your ambitions, your intelligence? Are you ready to trust your intuition and your instincts to find the new path for you to follow?

You will probably struggle with your thoughts and fears. But I am encouraging you to confront the obstacles. Move out of your corner—move into an area of change and adventure. Face making mistakes, and forgive yourself for being imperfect. Accept your failures *and* successes. Discover those feelings and attitudes you respond to and admire in others—emulate them and stretch to a new concept and realization of the wonder of being a woman. Don't permit the excuse of your children, your family, your responsibilities, or false guilt keep you from moving forward. My children are proud of who I have become. Rather than suffering from my demonstration of individuality, it has helped them to be themselves.

Don't forget you are nature's own creation, and like the tight bud of a flower, you already contain all your own lovely, positive qualities inside. It is far from vanity to nurture, protect, and encourage this unique identity.

Find out what kind of a flower you really are. You don't have to add petals. Let the ones you have unfold!

Like a dancer, you should put yourself in training to accomplish your goal of being happy, healthy, beautiful—and slim. Get food out of your thoughts if you want less of it in your body. Take the stand that you are in control—not only of your appetite but of your life.

Can you picture yourself as someone who craves refinement and moderation? If not, why not? Do you believe more in the temporary satisfaction of food than in the lasting fulfillment that is possible for your entire life? One half hour of time devoted to improving the way you think and feel about yourself can satisfy you more than any plateful of food. Try reading a book instead of having a cocktail. Play a game with your children instead of sitting down to a snack. Keep a light touch in your life: too much seriousness or intensity can produce a heavy heart and a heavier body.

When I go into training—a more positive image than dieting—I immediately go to the library and stock up on books. I make sure they are handy at all times. I train myself to reach for a book instead of reaching for food. In this way I not only control my weight but I add to the enrichment of my life. You may find your inspiration elsewhere: in painting, in writing, in photography, or in simply doing a good deed for someone else. There are hundreds of different ways to take your mind off food. Use them as aids to placing your eating in the context of a whole life-style.

In the beginning, you will have to follow a few simple guidelines at mealtimes. Try serving yourself half the portions you are used to. Since we eat with our eyes, you will probably have to retrain your eye to accept as "normal" an amount that may now appear to you as "skimpy." Use more imagination to present food more attractively. Try using luncheon plates until dainty quantities appeal to you aesthetically. Your stomach will settle for less food when your mind tells it to. As for the excessive food served in restaurants, your decision to control your own life makes more sense than giving in to the notion that it's a sin to "waste" food. It is far more important not to waste the potential of a life than not to waste the food on a plate.

We all want to see rapid results, but any training takes time and demands discipline. However, any person, at any age, can *retrain* her concepts about food, change her eating habits, and teach her stomach to feel satisfied. Incidentally, we need to stop equating lots of food with lots of energy! The harder I work physically, the less food I require. It is when I eat *more* than the simplest requirements of my body that I feel tired and sluggish.

Any doctor will tell you that you are healthier when you are thinner. Less weight means less burden for the heart, both physiologically and psychologically. Don't forget that your body's health depends on your mental and emotional harmony.

One of the most important areas to understand in our self-care is sex. So often it is unfulfilled and unresolved sexual desire that leads people to eat too much. The more you follow a regimen, like my method, that seeks to train both the body and the mind, the more relaxed and happy you will be with yourself. The more you are able to understand yourself, like yourself, and be proud of your body, the better a sexual partner you will be.

You know that you are sometimes going to feel hungry, restless, unfulfilled. So what? Who says you *always* have to be happy? Or satisfied? Hating yourself is worse! Change means being uncomfortable for awhile. So be uncomfortable! So be hungry! Your suffering will decrease as your mental strength and pride increase. There is no satisfaction from food or sex that can ever equal that of liking yourself.

Decide now to do whatever it takes to be proud of yourself. Put yourself on a program of healthy emotion. That is the most important and the only practical beginning to proper self-care.

△ The Apex
△ of the Triangle

One day, eight years ago now, I sat beside my bedroom window and looked across acres of smooth green lawns and suburban houses. Why did I feel so isolated from these surroundings—so isolated from life itself?

I had achieved the American dream—a handsome husband, lovely children, a ranch house, and two cars. Why was the dream more like a nightmare?

Feelings of dread persisted. I was afraid that my Midwest security was in fact a prison—with my husband and the church the keepers of the key. They made me feel guilty for even questioning the life I led. They thought I was "sick" for not being content with what I was and had. In fact, my questioning of values *did* make me ill.

During this time, I read *Women & Madness* by Phyllis Chesler and came across this passage about Zelda Fitzgerald: "Only if she does 'good work' can she defend herself against Scott's slighting comments. She says she is tired of being forced into accepting Scott's opinions and decisions about everything. In fact, she would not do so; she would rather be hospitalized."

Those words struck home. I knew I had to find inner freedom or I too would be in danger of destroying myself. As it was, I was having physical and emotional attacks that were terrifying—a pounding heart and everything inside me racing, as though there were some gas pedal being pushed hard into the floorboard of my being. I was too afraid to go to a doctor.

No one I turned to was able to help or understand, so finally I wrote out my own prescription for recovery. It said: "Leigh, your life belongs to you first. You are not going to give in, or give up. But to survive, you must, like the dancer that you were trained to be, exercise your inner strength and recapture your sense of self-worth. You must refuse to be depersonalized, manipulated, or helpless.

"Stand on your own two feet. Creating a better self-image is not going to create new abilities, talents, and powers, but it will release and utilize what is already there. Believe that what you believe in *is* worthwhile—that *you* are worthwhile."

As I began slowly to win some of my battles, I realized that indifference to the verdict of society was the only protection I had. When I was emotionally and physically a little stronger, I faced the fact that I did not love my husband nor agree with the influence of my church or its community. If I stayed where I was, I realized that not only would my own new strength be constantly tested but there was a danger that the potential of my children too would be crushed.

I left. I brought my children to New York and started a new life. Within five years I had a very successful business, a son and a daughter who are strong and happy, and supportive friends. My present life is filled with people and activities that enrich my life. I can look ahead and see a future of expansion—there is no more danger of contraction in my life.

A wonderful reward for anyone's courage to change is the realization that your new strength can become a source of strength for others. For me, each new step involving a new home, a new business, new students and friends became stepping stones of outreach and help to others. I am now very far from that window where once I merely looked out on life. I have traveled across the triangle's watery side of uncertainty and change—and reached out to the sky for the freedom and fullness of all that life has to offer.

△ Your Body
△ as a Work of Art

Now that you are going to approach your body as a work of art, I'd like to share with you the approach to life that Pavlova taught her students. "You must be an artist in your *life* before you can be an artist on the *stage*," she said. This was dinned into me over and over again as I grew up, but only in the last decade have I come to understand the full significance of her message and to value its practical wisdom.

An artist, according to the dictionary, is someone "who works with skill and good taste." Would you be happier living your life unskillfully with bad taste? If you would not, then you too must approach your life and work as an artist.

Have you given thought to the way you are approaching your world? An artist creates harmony out of chaos, demonstrates order where there is disorder, expresses inspiration and feeling where there is emptiness and coldness, and finally gives to the world more beauty and loveliness than he or she takes from it. An artist also creates from what is at hand—knowing that the "ideal" circumstance is seldom available.

I believe that it is the truth of this philosophy—this commitment to skill and good taste in every detail of my life—that taught me how to bring about beauty, health, and fulfillment not only for myself but for many others who accepted and practiced these principles and rules. Don't forget, it's not just the rules in this book but the *spirit* you express in the demonstration of those rules that will enable you too to say, "I am never too old; it is never too late—because I am an artist at living."

PART II

PART II

△ The Leigh Welles Class

After you have learned the importance of *mentally* visualizing the correct and lovely image you wish to bring out, you are ready to begin on the physical one. *But don't forget:* keeping the image in your mind is essential to producing it.

It is not just the quantity but the quality of the exercise that is going to count. A few exercises done well can change, firm, and strengthen. Many exercises done incorrectly can work against you. Work slowly, consistently, correctly, and you will build more strength than you ever thought possible. There is a tendency to hurry through exercises. Don't. Establish a rhythm as strict as if you had a metronome. Self-regulation is a skill, not a gift. You can learn it and practice it.

Anyone can do these exercises. Neither your age nor the condition of your body is a legitimate deterrent to your beauty and energy. Any woman, regardless of age and regardless of the figure she previously possessed, can experience a transformation. I am directing this book and my teaching at this transformation. It has already been accomplished for hundreds of women, and it can happen to you.

Now I am going to lead you through a class. Before we begin, I must assume you are in normal, good health. As a rule, we do not allow women who are greatly overweight to begin class but ask them to wait until they have demonstrated their desire to change by a gradual, but consistent, weight loss. In addition, it is impossible in a book to take every physical problem into account. Therefore, the reader must use her own good judgment and common sense while exercising. These exercises, performed correctly, cannot hurt you; but because they do produce results, they may, in the beginning, cause more muscular soreness than you are used to. This is a normal ache and disappears with repetition of the exercises. Each person's body is different, however, and where one student will feel the results of stretch immediately, another will not feel anything for months.

You should have a stationary object to hold onto

at approximately waist level. A kitchen sink is often the best support, but a bedpost or the knob of a closed door is adequate. This then becomes your ballet "barre."

The following pages contain two levels of classes. Perfect your technique and skill at Level I before attempting the Level II exercises. As your body gains strength and you are ready for a challenge, you can practice both levels of some of the exercises.

Do not force your body unduly. On the other hand, do not be afraid that your body is so fragile that it might break. No book can eliminate the need for the student to use her own common sense.

Your class work will consist of four parts: barre work, center work, jumping, and floor work. These exercises take into consideration the needs of *all* parts of the body. They are ordered and spaced in such a way that the weak or unused body will not be overtaxed or overstrained or become overdeveloped. Do not be afraid of getting big muscles. These exercises, based on Russian classical technique, produce the sleek legs of Russian-trained ballerinas, such as Makarova.

The way to build strength is to start with the first exercise and progress slowly, without stopping. If, in the beginning, you cannot work too long (and this is normal), do only as many exercises as you reasonably can, adding a little more each day as your stamina improves. Try not to stop or let down between the exercises but continue smoothly with the sequence. This enables the muscles and sinews to warm up properly and yield and stretch, while at the same time you build up the endurance necessary to make increasing demands on yourself. The sequence, continuity, exactness, and rhythm of these exercises are what make them unique and effective. Each exercise is carefully chosen and placed in sequence to produce both a demanding and relaxing process for the body. The rhythm of the exercise itself, combined with the flow of one exercise into the next, is one of the most vital ingredients of the success of this method and separates it from others. Practice each exercise according to the counts given to ensure the correct degree of effort and relaxation of the muscles. While this is a condensed class, the number of exercises, if practiced slowly, will ensure the right amount of work done on your own. Again, don't be afraid of becoming tired or having sore muscles; continued practice will soon eliminate that. But on the other hand, don't make the mistake of thinking you must feel exhausted or sore to be producing results. Progress is the result of consistent practice while using relaxed strength.

I must emphasize that the parts of the body cannot be isolated. What you do with the spine affects the legs; what you do with the legs affects the stomach. No single exercise is your panacea. They are all equally beneficial and important because you are made up of component parts sitting on top of one another. Don't think that concentrating your efforts on your thighs and ignoring your back will accomplish anything for your legs. An equalized strength, a controlled flexibility, a balanced approach to your work—these must be your aims.

The beginning of control lies in your awareness of your body, its muscles, and feelings. This, plus the following exercises, will enable you to redefine your body to your own liking.

 The Ballet Body

The following rules must be applied to all your work:

Your Mind:

- You must always be visualizing what you are working toward—continuously "drawing" improved mental images as you progress. Practice perceiving beneath the surface that new outline you wish to bring out.

Your Feelings:

- The secret to using the body properly is in learning to balance the right amount of effort with an equal amount of ease and relaxation. This principle is totally opposite to the "pain is gain" theory all too prevalent in modern exercise. When your feelings within are "at ease," your movements without will be too, which is the truest way to a healthy and fit body.

Your Body:

• The stomach muscles must be "pulled in and up" at all times and for all exercises. When they are *not*, you are nullifying the effect of the exercise. This may not be easy, but it must be done and can be done with time, effort, and patience.

• The seat must be pulled together and held together, regardless of what the legs are doing. If it is not, the fat of the seat and thighs will spread and get larger instead of smaller.

• The knees and thighs must be constantly and consistently pulled up. By that I mean that the kneecaps and the fatty part of the thighs must literally pull or lift upward. This may take you weeks, or months, before it happens, but until it does you are not completely stretching. Contrary to some opinions, you do not kick off, slap off, or shake off fat—you stretch off fat. Don't expect to build the strength that this requires in ten easy lessons. Nothing worth accomplishing ever happened fast. Regardless of your age or current condition, however, you can learn this principle, apply it, and eventually accomplish it.

• The body's weight must consistently be held slightly forward with the ribcage and chest ahead of your stomach.

• Smooth, controlled flow is the basis of safe and correct exercise. Every movement must be made with a steady rhythm, not syncopated jerks.

Mindless work leads to mistakes. Spiritless work causes the weight to press down. The ballet body is shaped by concentrating on upward thoughts and feelings.

The more you build a balance of flexibility and strength in your body, along with positive feelings in your heart, the greater are your chances to preserve and improve your health, youthfulness, and energy.

△ *Explanation of Terms*

Alignment of Leg:

The middle of the knee must always be centered over the middle of the foot; ankle and instep must be held up.

Alignment of Spine:

The spine must remain centered between the hips and stretched upward from the tailbone. The hip of the working leg must not be allowed to raise thereby throwing the spine out of alignment.

Barre:

A stationary horizontal support for preliminary exercises. A standard barre is attached on poles to the floor or on brackets to the wall and is approximately the height of your waist. A counter top, the knob of a closed door, or a chair back will do just as well.

Battements:

Kicks from the hip with the legs turned out, the knees straight, the toes pointed.

Center Work:

The next stage of development after the barre when similar exercises are done in the center of the room without the help of holding onto a barre. Strength and balance are stressed.

Positions of the feet for adults:

First position: heels together and touching, toes turned apart in a V.

Second position: feet in same V but heels apart approximately 12 inches.

Third position: the heel of one foot placed in front of the instep of the other foot, toes turned out.

Parallel: feet together, toes pointing straight ahead.

Floor Work:

Any exercise sitting or lying on the floor in which the floor is supporting you rather than your legs and spine.

Plié:

To bend the knees. In a correct plié the leg must bend so the knee goes forward over the middle of the foot. The body remains undisturbed on top of the legs without any adjustment of the spine or hips. If you bend and straighten your legs without adjusting (moving) the position of your torso, your spine will remain erect and your weight will stay on the balls of the feet.

Point:

A complete extension of the foot by arching the instep and pointing the toes—essential to the elongation of the muscles and sinew of the leg.

Port de bras:

Describes the "carriage of the arms" but also includes the movement of head, ribcage, and upper back. When used properly the arm, head, and upper torso present an appearance of grace and poise.

Relevé:

A stretching up as you rise up on the balls of your feet. Your knees remain straight as the heels lift off the floor. In order to balance at this "new height" you must feel your entire body forward over your toes.

Supporting leg:

Refers to the leg you are standing on when you lift the other leg off the floor. The supporting leg must remain firm and not shift as the "working leg" moves.

"To the side" or *second position:*

When you kick sideways both legs must remain turned out. That is, beginning in first position, both legs rotate outward as far as they can at the top of the legs. The feet should form a V. Then if you follow the line of the toes, it should lead the leg up slightly forward of the hip, and the leg will remain in the same position at the top of the kick: knee on top, heel forward, ahead of the toes. *The torso remains facing front.* Adults should not attempt to kick directly sideways, thereby twisting the spine.

Tendu:

To stretch the foot to an arched point on the floor, leg turned out, knee straight.

Turn out:

Refers to the ability of the thighs to turn away from center in the hip socket. To turn out your foot, you rotate the entire leg from the hip. When both legs turn out you will feel the muscles at the top of the legs rotate in opposite directions, the way the blades of an eggbeater turn.

Working leg:

Refers to the leg that is moving as opposed to the supporting leg, which is next to the barre.

△ The Barre Work

TO BEGIN

In the studio we have a barre, or horizontal pole, to hold onto. All you need is a stationary object at about waist height. This should be a light, secure support to steady you and not a crutch to substitute for the use of your own strength. Wear something feminine that won't interfere with your movement. It is vital to see yourself as a work of art in progress, and part of doing this is wearing clothing that makes you feel graceful and attractive. By feeling that way you begin to look that way.

It is important that the body be warmed up slowly to prevent strain. It is essential, therefore, that you practice the exercises in the following order to protect yourself from injuries that result from working with "cold muscles" or from unrealistic or excessive demands. By giving your body the careful conditioning of these exercises, you will discover a whole new way of working and feeling that will make you look better and feel stronger.

Place one hand on your support and let's begin. Practice each exercise on one side, then turn and repeat, holding on with the other hand.

FIRST POSITION EXPLAINED

First position is the starting position for many of these exercises so it is worth the time to learn it properly.

Stand with your heels together and rotate your legs slightly outward to form a V with your feet. The insides of your thighs are touching. The instep, or arch of the foot, is lifted; the inside ankle bone is held "up" and firm. The weight of the body is forward over the balls of the feet. Heels are touching the floor lightly. The entire spine is slightly forward with the weight of the torso lifting itself up and out of the hips. The abdomen is pulled in and up at the same time. The buttocks squeeze together and "lock." The knees, thighs, and seat stretch up—the fat literally lifting higher.

The free arm is held to the side, slightly ahead of the body, with the elbow and wrist lifted to create a smooth curve that is slightly below your shoulder. Shoulders should gradually drop and soften as the back muscles get stronger, and the back remains erect and straight without strain. The back of your head is in line with the spine; the facial muscles and jaw are relaxed.

Feel that your weight is balanced with 50 percent of it on each foot. Picture your spine as a flag pole, kept firm and straight by the balance of both legs. This feeling of balance must become instinctive—like a built-in meter that notifies you if you "tilt." Finally, do not hold your breath. Allow it to flow in and out. You should feel like a bird with her talons over the branch—poised for flight.

THE IMPORTANCE OF THE BALLET PLIÉ AND RELEVÉ

This basic ballet exercise is one of the most important to your body's needs. It is the oil for your machinery. The action of the plié and relevé gently warms up the muscles, sinews, and tendons so that they may stretch without harm. At the same time, they firm, tone, and smooth the skin and fat of your legs. Without this well-oiled flexibility, there is no grace, no real strength, and no ease. When this exercise is practiced daily, it will have a noticeable effect in elongating and refining your thighs and calves. Cellulite disappears as you learn to use your muscles to pull the skin taut at the top of your thighs. The demi-plié is also the best exercise to stretch the Achilles tendon—so vital to moving, running, and jumping.

The correctly practiced plié and relevé should elongate and slim the calf and thigh muscles. Calf muscles should *not* get hard or bigger. Thighs should *not* look muscular or "tough."

The relevé following each plié helps to "remind" the body to lift the pressure and weight out of the hips and legs and to release the energy out of the body. Each relevé adds to the strength of the thigh muscles until they can actually pull the weight of the fat up, thereby smoothing and slimming the leg.

Demi-plié

In the demi-plié, the center of the knee must bend directly in line with the middle of each foot. You must simultaneously "pull up" the inside ankle bone and keep the arch (or instep) of the foot from "rolling over" (or collapsing). Practicing the demi-plié strengthens the ankles and feet so that you can not only stand correctly but jump and run with correct alignment. The entire length of the spine remains straight and erect as you bend the knees.

Relevé

In the relevé, raise up on the balls of both feet, keeping the ankles firm, the weight centered over each foot. Do not allow the knees to flex as you rise, nor allow the kneecaps to drop as you smoothly and gently return the heels to the floor. If the ankle is kept from wavering and the leg is kept straight, you will build strength into your feet and ankles.

LEVEL I
Demi-plié in first position
(with relevés)

The demi-plié and relevé are a gentle introduction of your body to movement, but tremendously important to the proper maintenance of your legs.

REMEMBER: Keep your chest lifted, your abdomen in and up. When done correctly you will not feel very much happening. Just as an oven barely gives off heat when you first turn it on, so it is with your body. Be patient! You are learning a new way to feel exercised.

For practice:
Repeat 8 times. Turn around and start over.

Begin in first position:

1. Bend the knees outward. Keep the heels on the floor, and the inside ankle bones "lifted up" to prevent the arch of the instep from collapsing. Keep the spine erect. 3 counts.

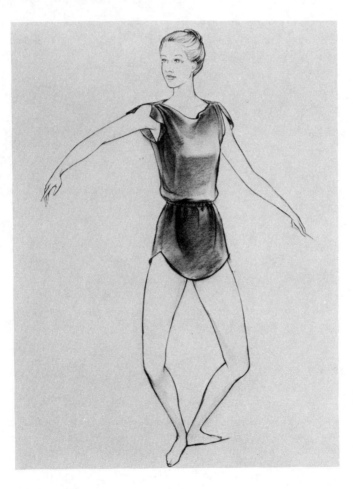

2. Straighten the knees, pulling up the kneecaps and stretching the muscles of the thighs upward. Keep the buttocks held firmly together. 3 counts.

3. Relevé. Raise your heels off the floor *without* flexing your knees. Spread weight equally over all 10 toes. Raise your arm and look up simultaneously. 3 counts.

4. Lower heels gently, feeling body is suspended in space, not sitting back on heels. Continue "pulling up" the knees. Arm returns to side. 3 counts.

LEVEL II
Grands Pliés

The grand plié is the continuation of the demi-plié. By going lower, the insides of the thighs are stretched more, and there is a loosening effect in the groin area. A plié is not a squatting movement, as some people mistakenly perform it, but a highly technical exercise that takes considerable practice to perform correctly.

REMEMBER: Your spine—from tailbone to collarbone—must remain straight. Visualize a straight line coming up out of the floor between your heels, and like an elevator, your plié descends and ascends on that line. Do not allow your seat to drop below the level of your knees when they are bent nor remain more than a second at the bottom of the grand plié. If you do, this can cause undue pressure on the knees. If you keep the plié flowing and smooth, it is beneficial. If you don't perform it correctly, you may wonder why your legs or knees hurt.

For practice:
  1 grand plié, 1 relevé. Repeat 8 times. The correct timing for the grand plié is

very important and should be done in the following manner:

Begin in first position:

> 3 counts for the demi-plié.
> 3 counts for the continuation of the grand plié.
> 3 counts returning to the demi-plié (heels are back on the floor).
> 3 counts straightening the knees.

The relevé should take the next 3 counts (place your arm over your head and stretch the whole body up toward the ceiling).

> 3 counts poised "in space."
> 3 counts as you lower the heels back to the floor (the arm opens to the side simultaneously).
> 3 counts pause (recheck tightness of seat and placement of weight).

As you bend your knees, make sure your arches are held up. The knees and thighs must open backward—the heels pushing lightly into the floor. (This stretches the Achilles tendon.) When you can't go any lower, slowly allow the heels to come off the floor, *as you push open your thighs.* Your seat and spine should be in a straight line. To come up from the grand plié, press your heels once more into the floor. Only *after* they are well placed should you allow your knees to straighten. To straighten the legs before the heels are down on the floor puts too much pressure on the calves, and instead of slenderizing the legs, you would create a hard, muscular look in the calves.

LEVEL I
Pliés in second position

In this wide-open position of the legs, an additional stretch is experienced in the inner thighs.

For practice:
   8 slow pliés. Turn around and start over.

   Begin in second position with feet about 12 inches apart:

1. Bend your knees directly over your toes, but DO NOT allow heels to come off floor. Keep your seat in a direct line between your feet, back perfectly straight. 6 counts.

2. Straighten the knees slowly, pulling kneecaps up and lifting thigh muscles by pulling upward. The seat should squeeze tightly together to sustain this. 6 counts.

REMEMBER: While you plié, the whole position of the body must stay erect as if there were a wall behind you. At the same time your knees and thighs are pushing backward against it.

LEVEL II
Introducing Third Position

In third position, the heel of one foot is placed in front of the middle of the other foot. Both legs and feet remain turned out. This position enables you to feel an even tighter grip between the thighs and seat. Fifth position, when the heel of one foot is crossed all the way over to the toe of the

other, is absolutely not necessary for any adult body and causes a great deal of unnecessary damage when—through ignorance or carelessness—it is forced. Anyone who has previously done any ballet as a child must remember that ballet is a technique developed for the flexibility and malleability of a young child's body. It was conceived and developed as a physical discipline that requires practice *every day*. For the adult who exercises two or three times a week, ballet is an entirely different matter and thus requires the modified technique I have developed for my classes. The adult does not need to achieve a complete "turn-out" to derive the benefits of ballet.

I have adapted the following ballet techniques to serve the needs of the *adult* body. These do not force your body into unnatural positions but attempt only what is physiologically correct and safe.

LEVEL II
Grand Pliés in third position

The same rules that pertain to first position apply here.

REMEMBER: The grand plié is the continuation of the demi-plié. Likewise, in coming back up from the grand plié, you must be sure to put the heels down BEFORE you straighten the knees. The open arm may lower with the plié and continue forward and up above your head with the relevé, giving you a feeling of continuous flow and rhythmical harmony. Remember that the idea is to learn to move well and *feel* graceful. You must be willing to believe in your femininity as you move.

For practice:

Begin in third position:

    1 grand plié, 1 relevé. Repeat 8 times.

    Use the same timing as you did for the grand plié in first position.

The thighs must be pushed open, or backward as you go lower but not at the expense of the straightness of your spine. The goal is to keep the back straight and balanced evenly between both legs while keeping the seat firmly together. Again, do not remain *in* the plié, but go down and come up smoothly without a pause.

LEVEL I
Battements tendus to the front
(stretching and lifting the leg)

This exercise provides the training ground for strengthening the stomach and back muscles and teaches you the correct way to move your legs as well. Tendus are done slowly and repetitively so they establish a correct habit of "feel" in the muscles. It is the consistent stretch of the entire leg while it is in motion that produces a refining and slimming result. It is the consistent stretching upward of the spine while the leg is in the air that produces the strength. The harder you point your toes, the more stretch you will feel in the thighs.

REMEMBER: Both legs must stay turned out at all times. This means your knees will be pointing sideways, away from each other with the feet in a V. When the leg is raised to the front, the knee is pointing to the side of the room. The working leg is always the one away from the barre. The supporting leg is always the one next to the barre.

For practice:

8 times to the front. Turn around and start over.

Begin in first position:

1. Slide the heel forward until the foot is stretched ahead with all the toes slightly touching the floor while the heel is forced up toward the ceiling. 2 counts.

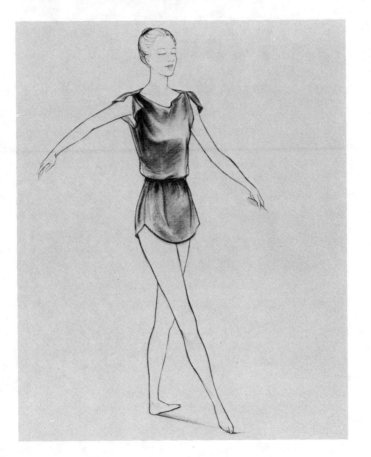

2. Lift the leg in front of you, knees and ankles stretched, toes pointed. Try to lift the torso off the supporting leg at the same time. 2 counts.

3. Control the fall of the leg by using the strength in your back. The toes gently touch, the ankle fully stretched, knee straight. 2 counts. Slide foot back to first without bending the knees. Stretch the weight up on supporting leg so the working leg will "fit." 2 counts.

LEVEL II
Battements tendus to the back

After you have learned to keep your hips squarely placed, you may add battements tendus to the back. It is not easy to lift the leg behind you while keeping the entire torso facing straight ahead. Care must be taken not to twist the torso sideways. As you lift the leg, the entire body should incline slightly forward so there is no unnatural strain placed on the lower part of the back.

REMEMBER: You are training your legs— especially the knees—to remain totally straight while you kick. The seat remains tight, the spine stretched forward with the chest lifted. Make an extra effort to straighten the knee as the leg lifts off the floor behind you. Again, keep the knee straight as you slide it back to first position. Keep both legs turned out.

For practice:
    8 battements tendus to the back.

Begin in first position:
  Slide the foot to a point back, lift the leg, point on the floor behind you, close to

first position. The free arm should be lifted in front of you, stretching the fingers toward the wall ahead of you.

Give 2 counts to each movement.

LEVEL I
Battements tendus to the side (extending and lifting the leg)

REMEMBER: When you kick the leg to the side, the center of the knee is pointing to the ceiling. Keep the foot fully pointed. The supporting knee does not bend, the spine remains straight. If the torso sinks or your back buckles in the middle, you are kicking too high.

For practice:

8 times to the side. Turn around and start over.

Begin in first position:

1. Slide the foot in the direction the toes are facing, until the foot is fully stretched and pointed to the side. 2 counts.

2. Lift the leg, keeping both thighs turned out. 2 counts.

3. Gently lower the leg to the floor with foot still pointed. 2 counts.

4. Slide foot back to first position. 2 counts.

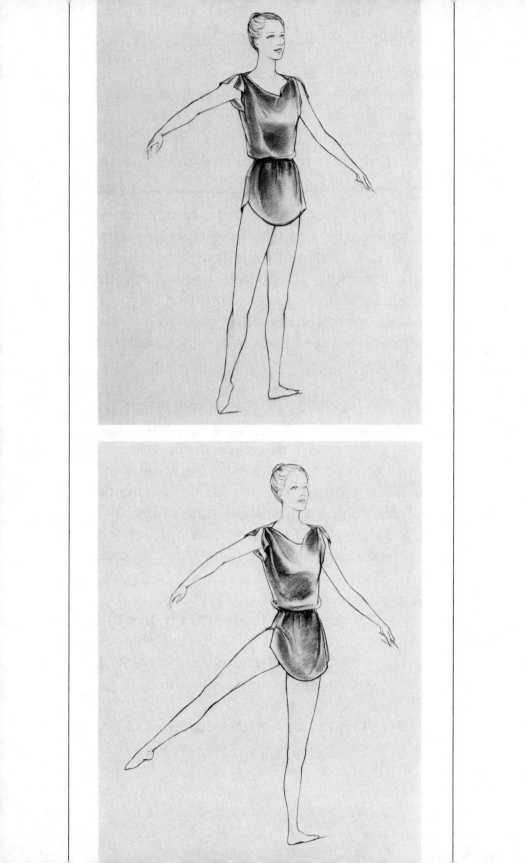

LEVEL II
Battements tendus en croix

Take the time to practice this properly as it is one of the most important preliminary exercises to the correct performance of a kick. If done properly, it can achieve the slimming result you want for your thighs and the strength you need for your back. It will also do wonders for the strengthening of your stomach muscles if you contract them forcefully with each kick.

REMEMBER: Do the number that is right for you. Start with 4 in each direction (16 in all) and repeat if you are still pulling your weight forward and off your seat. Try to feel the stretch on the inside of the thigh and the tightening of the seat on the outside. Point the toes and stretch the knees and ankles as much as you can.

For practice:

4 battements tendus to the front.
4 battements tendus to the side.
4 battements tendus to the back.
4 battements tendus to the side.
Repeat.

Give one count to each movement of the leg.

GRANDS BATTEMENTS
EXPLAINED

This exercise, when learned and practiced correctly, will take inches off your hips and thighs, strengthen your back, and exercise your abdominal muscles. But please believe me, there is only one correct way to "kick" off fat and that is the grands battements as they are taught in Russian classical technique. Once and for all you must banish the notion that the higher you kick, the more you are accomplishing. If the back "buckles" while you kick—even the slightest movement in the spine—you are allowing the weight of your torso to press down into your hips, and you are spreading your seat and forcing your stomach out! This will, of course, ultimately make your thighs larger instead of smaller. It is NOT the height of the kicked leg; it is the correctness of the kick, i.e., the stretch upward of the supporting leg and the lift of the torso that produces the slimming and trimming result to the legs. A battement is not a gimmick to throw yourself ignorantly into. It is a highly technical and profoundly effective exercise that takes knowledge and practice to perfect.

LEVEL I
Grands battements

The grand battement goes through the same positions as the battement tendu but does not stop on the floor. Learn to swing the leg up and down with strength, control, and freedom.

REMEMBER: The knee of the supporting leg *must not flex*, and the spine and torso *must not sink*. Kick lower if that happens. Don't raise the hip of the working leg. Don't forget to tighten the buttocks with every kick. Your musicality is always important but especially so here. Like a pendulum, the swing should be continuous and smooth.

For practice:
    8 kicks to the front, 8 kicks to the side. Repeat twice; 32 kicks in all. Turn around and start over.

Begin in first position:

1. To the front. Keeping both legs turned out and knees straight, swing the working leg up—the center of the knee should be pointing to the side of the room. 3 counts as it swings up and 3 counts as it returns to first position.

2. To the side. As you kick sideways be sure the center of the knee points toward the ceiling. It is important to keep the stomach facing forward and not let it turn sideways with the leg. 3 counts up and 3 counts down to first position. Make sure both knees remain straight and stretched at all times, the foot arched or pointed as forcefully as possible.

LEVEL II
Grands battements en croix

If you have learned to keep the balance of your body equally placed on both legs while you kick, you may take your battements from third position. When you kick to the side, alternate the placing of your foot first in front and then in back of the supporting leg. Both feet and legs remain turned out throughout the exercise.

REMEMBER: Give priority to the quality of the kick—not the height. If your supporting knee flexes, you have sacrificed the slimming effect to your thighs. If you allow your spine to "settle" you have sacrificed building strength in your back. Hold onto your mental image of the flagpole through your spine. After each kick try to place just a little more weight on the front foot. This extra effort will protect you from gradually settling back on your seat and hips. Don't forget, the more arched the foot and straighter the knee of the working leg, the quicker and surer the result.

For practice:

Begin in third position:

> 8 battements to the front.
> 8 battements to the side.
> 8 battements to the back.
> 8 battements to the side.

Rhythm is always essential and helps avoid strain to the muscles from uneven work. Count one beat for the leg to go up and one count for it to come back to the floor.

LEVEL I
Forward port de bras

This lovely exercise is fun to do and beautiful to watch. When practiced correctly, it will stretch the back of the thighs, tighten the stomach, and both relax and elongate the spine. But most of all, it should give you the joy of feeling your body move, bend, stretch like a dancer's.

REMEMBER: Keep the entire exercise moving smoothly and rhythmically. Imagine that you are descending to the floor of the ocean, then raising your head high above the waves.

For practice:
 8 times. Turn around and start over.

Begin with feet parallel:

1. Bend forward, knees straight, reaching toward the floor in front of you. Turn your chin toward your chest. Pull stomach up inside your body. Keep buttocks tight. Do not allow your seat or legs to move backwards. 6 counts.
 Roll up the spine. 6 counts.

2. Keep inside of thighs together and relevé, continuing a circle with the arm until it is overhead. Without allowing your knees, thighs, or stomach to go forward, slightly arch backward, letting the arm lead. 6 counts.

3. Gently open and drop the arm to the side as you lower the heels and return to original starting position. 6 counts.

LEVEL II
Forward port de bras en relevé

Standing in third position with both legs and feet turned out equally and with hips squarely placed and parallel to the front of the room, repeat Level I. With one leg in front of the other you should be able to grip the seat and inner thighs even tighter. The secret lies in maintaining this "tightness" *as much as you possibly can* as you bend forward. This exercise will only slim and stretch you IF you work against the pull of the seat and legs to separate.

REMEMBER: Try to keep a little more of the body weight on the front foot at all times. (Try it both ways, and you will feel the difference.) Don't bend over so far that you sacrifice the tightness of your seat. You won't be able to go down very far, if you are doing this properly. Suppleness is the result of months of careful practice. Force it and you are working against yourself. You may not like finding out how rigid you are, but the cost of fooling yourself is too high a price to pay.

For practice:

Begin in third position:

Repeat 4 times. The feet remain on the floor as you bend down and come back up. The heels raise in the relevé when the arm is over your head.

Now repeat 4 more times, this time staying on the balls of your feet (heels off the floor) throughout. Move the front foot so the ankle of the front leg is touching and "locked" together with the ankle of the back leg. Keep it this way as you bend over toward the floor. Try not to drop the heels. Roll the back up. Stretch upward and try to look a little farther behind you each time. Keep your seat tight, your stomach pulled in. You must find a visual image that conveys a feeling of relaxed strength to you. How about the yawn of a lion? Keep the rhythm smooth, your feelings expansive.

LEVEL I
Balançoire

This swinging motion of the leg is easy and fun. The continuous action forward and back helps loosen the leg in the groin, allowing freer and more effective movement.

REMEMBER: Even though the torso leans slightly forward and back to add forceful-ness to your kicks, the spine should still remain stretched out. Do not turn side-ways when the leg goes to the back. Allow the toes to touch the floor first as the leg descends and stretch the entire leg fully when lifted each time.

For practice:
Swing forward and back 16 times. Begin in a lunge position: back leg straight, front knee bent, both legs turned out. As you swing the leg forward and up, straighten the supporting knee, keeping it straight for the 16 swings front and back. Try to go a little higher with each swing. Keep the working leg turned out all the time. Count a fast 1, 2, 3 with each swing of the leg.

LEVEL II
Balançoire (continued)

Like a football player aiming for the goal posts, learn to make a strong but controlled movement from beneath the hips.

REMEMBER: Do not allow your torso (or stomach) to turn sideways as you swing the leg. The hips remain stationary. The leg must move beneath the hip bone, otherwise you are not stretching the inside of the leg. As the leg swings to the back, allow the torso to go slightly forward. Keep stretching both knees, especially as the leg swings to the back. The tendency is to let the knees relax. Don't. In your attempt to kick higher, do not allow the spine to bend. Remember to visualize that space between each vertebra and keep elongating the spine to keep it that way. It is never worth compromising a spine or spreading a seat to get a leg higher.

For practice:
Beginning from the lunge position, swing the leg forward—keeping both legs turned out—and straightening the supporting leg as you kick. 3 counts.
Return to the lunge. 3 counts.

Repeat this swing forward and return to the lunge. 3 counts front and 3 counts back.

Now, swing leg front and back and front; then go back to the lunge. 12 counts. (The supporting leg straightens during these three swings and remains so until you return to the lunge.)

Repeat from the beginning 4 times.

Continue a 1, 2, 3 rhythm throughout.

LEVEL I
Thigh lifts (attitude kicks)

The thighs are the heaviest part of the body to move, so they have to be coaxed into action. The momentum gained through lifting them, with a swinging upward thrust, helps you overcome their weight and eventually makes them feel lighter. And when they feel lighter and move more freely, they will become lighter. Practiced consistently, thigh lifts will eventually help overcome their thickness.

REMEMBER: All the rules for grands battements apply equally here. The only difference is that you are bending the working knee very slightly in order to get the leg a little higher and stretch the inner thighs a little more. Do not lean back or shift sideways. Keep your seat tight and the supporting leg straight.

For practice:
   4 to the front, 4 to the side; repeat 4 times; 32 in all. Turn around and start over.

Begin in first position:

1. Forcefully throw up the leg in front of you, bending the working knee sideways and raising the heel with the foot pointed. Return to first. 2 counts up, 2 counts down.

2. With a strong upward thrust, raise the leg sideways, knee slightly bent, pointing the toes downward. Don't bend the knee too much. Try to feel the stretch at the top and inside of the thigh. Return to first. 2 counts up, 2 counts down.

LEVEL II
Thigh lifts (continued)

The hard part here is to keep the hips from moving and consequently throwing your spine off center. However, if you line up your body with something straight in front of you or visualize your spine as an immovable flagpole, you should be able to achieve a measure of the necessary balance and eventual ease that is needed. Don't overlook the powerful help of your back muscles. Just because you can't see them doesn't mean they're not there just waiting to be put to work—and strengthened. You'll find them by expanding your ribcage both front and back.

REMEMBER: Students usually err on the side of bending the raised leg too much. But then you don't feel as much stretch along the inner thigh. Think of it as an almost straight leg kick, but in order to lift it higher you "cheat" a little by flexing the knee a bit. Don't lean back—rather, try to move your chest forward toward your leg. If you find you begin to wobble on the supporting leg, stop. Better to do fewer that are correct—and gradually increase the number—than to begin to create a pattern of sloppy habits.

For practice:

Begin in first position:

4 thigh lifts to the front, 4 to the side, 2 to the front, 2 to the side, 1 to the front, 1 to the side, 1 to the front, 1 to the side.

Repeat this combination at least twice.

Count these lifts out loud as you do them. This should give you about the right tempo. It should be brisk but not hurried.

LEVEL I
Side port de bras and stretch (Step 1)

This exercise slims the waist by stretching the body up and out of it. It also includes a contraction of the stomach muscles, in a grip and release method, that helps to build the muscles back from their softness and flabbiness. Allow yourself to feel graceful and move like a dancer.

REMEMBER: You are drawing semi-circles in space (step 1), then cutting through the center of your circle with a straight line (step 2). Try to follow those images with your eyes, literally seeing the line you draw in space. This will help your neck and head to move and relax some of its tension. Don't be surprised if this is difficult in the beginning. The muscles of the eyes and neck are usually quite stiff.

For practice:
    8 times. Turn around and start over.

Begin with feet parallel on balls of your feet:

1. Lean sideways away from your barre, opening the free arm sideways in an arc up over the head and reaching with the fingers to the ceiling over the barre. Don't let the waist collapse on either side but stretch it up and out of the hips. Keep your legs together. 6 counts. Reverse the arc, bringing the arm back to your side and lower the heels to the floor. 6 counts.

2. Bring your free hand between your breasts, fingers pointed toward the ceiling, as you extend the hand toward the ceiling until the arm is straight with hand above and in front of head, face looking up toward hand. Rise on your toes as your hand goes up. 6 counts.

3. Drop slowly into a semi-crouched position, your seat underneath you. Keep your knees together, the head and torso forward. Allow arm bending at the elbow to slowly fall by your side to floor. In bending the body, contract the stomach muscles forcefully and swiftly as though you had been hit in the stomach with a softball. At the same time, the rest of movement moves slowly. 6 counts. Slowly roll back up to the beginning position, the head being the last to lift. The heels come down as you raise up. 6 counts. Remain in beginning position for 6 counts while you retighten your seat and make sure your weight is forward.

LEVEL II
Side port de bras (Step 2)

This is a continuation of the preceding exercise allowing still more movement of the body. Your entire "being" should be involved. You are drawing more circles in space. Picture them!

REMEMBER: The average adult body is stiff in its head, eye, and neck movements. There is opportunity in this for a lot of workout, but in the beginning you must force these parts of your body to move. As the arm swings behind you, let the head and shoulders drop backward also. Look up at the ceiling until you see your hand reach its ultimate height over your head. The head and shoulders create the slight arch backward—not the spine or stomach. Make a concentrated effort to tighten the seat and pull the stomach in at all times. As you bend forward, continuing to stretch toward the floor, allow the head to roll under toward your chest. The knees are straight throughout this segment; the legs are held tightly together. When you have mastered the technique of this exercise, use it to "indulge" your innermost desire to let go and enjoy your body.

For practice:

Repeat the side port de bras Level I exercise once. Now continue it by raising your arm straight ahead in front of you and relevé onto the balls of your feet. Drop the arm (not the heels) and let it circle backward, upward, and over your head, and continue this circle down to the floor. Lower the heels, keeping the knees straight, and slowly roll the spine back up to the starting position. Start over from the very beginning.

Repeat 4 to 8 times.

Continue to count with the same rhythmical flow as in Level I. Think of a languorous waltz.

LEVEL I
Battements facing center

I used this exercise to take inches off my thighs, but it must be done accurately, or it won't work. You must have the whole torso well forward feeling as though you are lifting off the top of the supporting leg with each kick. Begin in first position with your back to the barre, holding on behind you. Do not allow either knee to bend at any time. If your whole body is pitched slightly forward from your heels, you will feel the stretch up the back of your thighs.

If the supporting leg buckles or any part of the spine moves as you kick, you must lower the kicking leg. *Height is not important.* Accuracy is.

Balance your weight at all times. Visualize a straight line going through the center of your head, through the spine, and between your feet. As you kick, keep your spine in line with that image.

For practice:
32 kicks in all, 2 with each leg.

1. To the front. Kick straight ahead with the leg turned out, the foot strongly pointed. Return to first. The second kick is stronger and higher. 2 counts up, 2 counts down.

For practice:
32 kicks in all, 2 to each side.

2. To the side. Visualize stretch: try thinking of a piece of elastic. Would anything happen to it if it went in one direction only? Stretch means opposition—something pulling two different ways at the same time. This is the principle that took off my fat and can take off yours too. Here is how you apply that principle in these kicks.

When you kick to the right side "pull" the left side of the body in the other direction, i.e., try to rotate the upper part of the left leg and the left side of the body away from and in the opposite direction to the right side, like two revolving doors going different ways. This creates the essential two-way stretch. The seat should be very tight. Don't shift your weight.

LEVEL II
Battements facing the barre

Battements are always harder to the back. There is a tendency to either raise the hip with the leg, which creates a "crimp" in the lower portion of the spine, or to allow the seat to loosen in an attempt to get the leg higher than your present technical skill permits.

REMEMBER: Be sure that your hips are "square" and remain so. Make an extra effort to squeeze the buttocks tightly together as you kick the leg. Visualize two straight lines—one that goes down through your body like a flagpole between your legs keeping you from tilting sideways; the other an imaginary line through your torso that stretches forward and up through your spine at an angle slightly ahead of you. The whole of your body inclines at a slight angle forward. This will prevent any strain to the lower back.

For practice:
Begin in first position:

32 kicks to the back alternating after 2 kicks with each leg. Count with the same tempo as Level I.

LEVEL I
Forward stretch and arch

The first part of this exercise creates suppleness; the second part stretches and strengthens the spine.

REMEMBER: You must always try to visualize what is happening inside your body. As you go forward, the spine is releasing and lengthening, while the stomach "disappears" inside. On returning to an upright position, the vertebrae are rolling up, one at a time, like heavy beads. In the arch backward, the entire body is creating one unbroken curve, the vertebrae at the small of the back continuing to stay separated by a cushion of space between each one.

For practice:
   8 times.

Begin with the feet parallel, holding onto the barre in back of you.

1. Slowly bend forward toward the floor, chin on chest; stomach pulled in; weight leaning forward away from barre. 6 counts.

2. Smoothly roll the spine back up to straight position. 6 counts.

3. Relevé, heels raised as high as possible, spine straight, knees pulled up, and legs together. Keep stomach flat and seat tight. The eyes and head go back. 6 counts.

4. Return to beginning position. 6 counts.

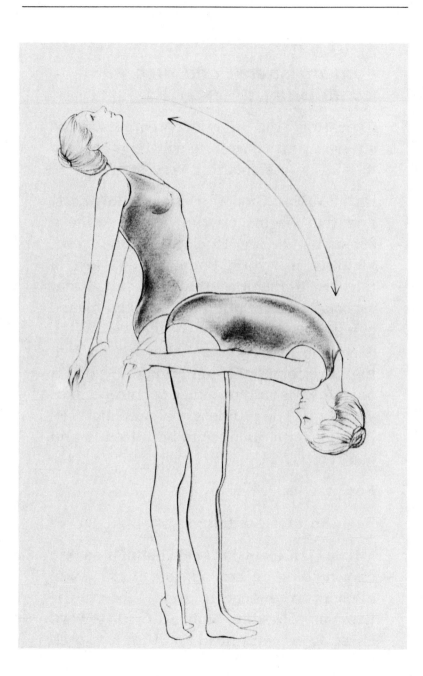

LEVEL II
Forward stretch and arch (continued)

Repeating this in relevé requires more strength and control. It will be necessary to hold onto something very stable.

REMEMBER: Smoothness is the key here, and that begins on the inside. Allow a sensuous feeling to flow through you, yielding up your body to the joy of release. Remember that any art form, especially one relating to the body, means emotional expression coupled with the execution of technique. Allowing no feeling to come through makes you a machine. Having no skill or control makes you inept. The ultimate goal, and satisfaction, is in the balance of both feeling and control.

For practice:

Begin in first position:

Relevé. Raise your heels as high as you can, holding on behind you. Bend down, allowing your head to get as close to the floor as possible, chin turned toward chest. Relax your head and turn it to each side slowly. Look at your stomach, checking to see that it has "disappeared" inside your body. Using the strength of the abdominal muscles—like the cogs of a wheel—pull or "wind" your back up to a straight position. Don't let your heels drop. Holding on in the most comfortable manner behind you and straightening your elbows, lean forward as far as you can go. Lead with your breasts, NOT your stomach. Allow your head and shoulders to fall backward. Open your mouth slightly allowing the jaw to relax. Look up and back. Lift your head and return to first position. Keep your seat very tight, or you will lose control.

Repeat 8 times, allowing the heels to come down between each one. Try humming a slow waltz allowing your movements to flow with it in a graceful, continuous manner.

△ The Center Work

By now your muscles should be warm and flexible, capable of working without any support. The center work—or work done in the middle of the room away from the barre—is designed to increase the demand on your body and build up increasing muscle strength and balance while continuing to stretch and reshape the legs and torso.

These exercises are familiar to most people. The important difference in this class is in learning to do them correctly so they also change and improve the physical appearance of your entire body, not just exercise the individual parts. You must know and apply very basic rules or the exercise is invalidated and only contributes to the problems of your physical appearance instead of helping it. If an exercise, done correctly, changes the structure of your body beneficially (and it does), then the same exercise, done incorrectly, changes it detrimentally. No exercise is done in a vacuum.

Remember that one of the secrets to stretching and in turn to thinning the body is achieved by getting and keeping the temperature of the inner and outer body warm. Therefore, I must again remind you not to stop between these exercises. You must begin at the beginning and continue straight through without letup. If your stamina lags in the middle, cut down on the number of times you repeat the exercises, but try to do some of all of them. The body responds beautifully to routine. Try to establish that routine and stick to it. Your rewards will soon appear in increased energy and a new sense of well-being.

LEVEL I
Relevés

The older I get, the more I see the importance and value of strong ankles and
flexible feet. And they will not stay strong
and flexible without specific exercises.
Don't do them and you may, one day,
wonder why you feel clumsy or unsteady
on your feet. It won't be age. It will be
lack of proper use and exercise.

REMEMBER: If you have been out of
shape, you will feel this exercise in
the calves. Persisting will eventually
strengthen the ankles and legs and eliminate any strain. Hold on to something if
you need to steady yourself. Don't be
alarmed by any creaking noises from your
ankles or knees. You are not hurting
them—but it does mean you need the "oiling" effect of these exercises.

For practice:
8 relevés with feet parallel. 8 relevés
with feet turned out in first position.

1. Rise up on the balls of your feet,
heels off the floor as high as possible.
Keep toes spread flat; don't curl them.

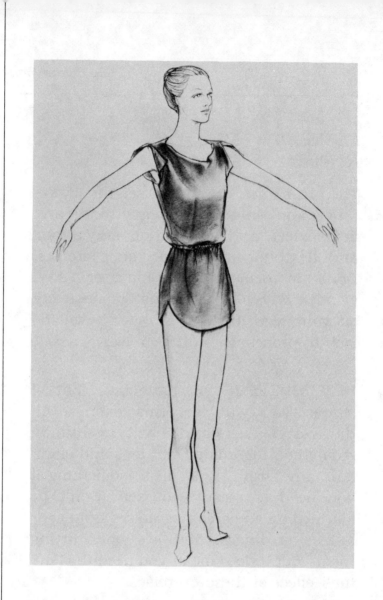

Keep the knees straight and the thighs stretched upward. Hold the seat tightly together. 3 counts.

2. Lower the heels gently, feeling as though you left your body suspended in space. 3 counts.

LEVEL II
Walking, waltzing, running

Try these simple routines to strengthen your legs and increase your stamina.

REMEMBER: Awkwardness is no one's personal possession. Everyone is awkward when they don't have the necessary knowledge or practice in some area. Grace is not a gift—it's a skill acquired by knowledge and practice.

For practice:
Use any tempo as long as it is steady. Try varying it, sometimes going slower, sometimes faster.

1. Tiptoe. Walk 8 steps forward on the balls of your feet. Drop your heels and walk back naturally for 8 steps. Repeat several times.

2. Pedal. Again, go forward, but this time as you tiptoe allow each foot to roll down from the ball of the foot to the heel. Try to have the knee straight when you step forward on the ball of the foot, and allow it to relax and bend as you come down. Pedal forward 8 times and walk back naturally 8 steps. Repeat several

times. Now, waltzing forward, drop one foot and go forward twice on tiptoe. Continue in a circle.

3. Using this same pedaling motion, run in place. Gradually begin to lift your knees higher and higher, adding as much bounce to it as you can. Be careful to continue the pedaling motion each time you land. Don't lean back. Keep your chest forward.

4. Run forward in a circle reaching ahead with the toes of each foot. Continue the same rolling effect as each foot lands. Spring off each leg, as you forcefully stretch the next foot forward. Head forward into your stride.

Be sure you always bend your knees when you land.

LEVEL I
Cross stretch

When practiced correctly, this exercise gives you a good feeling of "pull" or stretch across the abdomen. The secret is in keeping the hips still and letting the *upper* torso do the turning. Don't be surprised if there is not much "give" in the beginning. It will come. At all times you are training yourself to move as a lithe, female jaguar—sleek, graceful, and powerful.

REMEMBER: The most important rule to remember here is NOT to allow the seat or legs to move backward as you bend over. The goal is to stretch the back of the thighs and buttocks, not touch the floor, so if the body begins to shift behind your heels, don't bend any farther. Be patient. It takes time and practice for the body to begin to yield up its tightness. You cannot "will" it into shape. You will only cultivate bad and costly habits by forcing "progress."

For practice:
   16 times.

Begin in second position with arms overhead in an open V.

Bend forward with the right fingers
reaching out ahead of your left foot—as
far forward as you can. Retrace the line
back up to starting position and repeat to
the other side. The seat will try to separate. Don't let it. Pull the stomach in
strongly as you go toward the floor. 6
counts over and 6 counts up.

LEVEL II
Cross stretch with parallel arms

Why do some people, practicing the same exercises, look better? Why are some getting thinner or stronger or straighter?

The difference is determined by your knowledge of the technique involved and your consistent application of the proper skills.

Try this exercise after you have absorbed all the rules for Level I.

For practice:

Keeping both arms totally stretched and parallel, repeat the Level I exercise. This time reach as far ahead of the left foot as you can with both hands. When your hands reach the floor, allow the head to continue until your chin is on your chest. Pull the tummy inside until it disappears. The back should be very rounded. Press the right heel into the floor and *do not allow your weight to shift to the left side.* Don't forget that the seat must not be allowed to move backward as you bend over. Yes, this is possible to control!

Now, with the arms stretched and parallel, swing back up to the starting position, and continue smoothly over to the other foot. Do not shift your weight onto the right foot—keep it evenly balanced between both. Press the heel of the left foot into the floor. *Be sure you constantly pull the thighs up.* If you don't pull the thigh muscles up and keep your seat tight, you may be one of those students asking why you don't get the beneficial results someone else does.

LEVEL I
Battements—flexed

The person who has learned to keep her weight out of her hips can kick the legs freely and forcefully, without shifting her weight or moving her spine. By using the valuable back muscles to maintain this balance while she kicks, the student contributes to the overall strength of her body. The flexed foot helps to "pull" or stretch the inside of the thighs.

REMEMBER: All the rules you applied at the barre must be reinforced at this point.

Feel the tummy pull in and up at the same time the leg lifts. Do *not* allow the spine to buckle nor the supporting knee to flex.

For practice:
32 kicks to the front, 4 with each leg.
32 kicks sideways, 4 with each leg.

Begin in first position:

1. Kick 4 times to the front with each leg, the heel pushing forward, foot flexed, legs turned out, each kick a little higher than the last. Do NOT lean back or allow the supporting knee to move. Lift your entire torso higher as you kick. 1 count. Control the fall of the leg as it returns to first position after each kick. 1 count.

2. Kick sideways, 4 times with each leg. Keep the hips still. Turn both legs outward away from each other evenly. The seat must stay pulled together whether the leg is in first position or in the air. Don't shift from side to side. 1 count up. 1 count down.

LEVEL II
Battements—balancing

This requires the use of your back muscles in order to keep your balance. Take a deep breath and open or expand your ribcage, duplicating this feeling in your back. You must keep the supporting leg completely straight throughout. If the knee bends or if the body moves, kick lower.

REMEMBER: Do not allow your seat to separate, or you will lose control. Keep both arms out to the side—slightly ahead of your body. Try to make sure that both legs are turned equally. As you swing the leg front, "lead" forward with the heel as you bring it through first position, but point it as you raise it in front. As you swing the leg back, "pull" the toes backward. The goal is a "centered" spine at all times, leaning neither to the right nor to the left.

For practice:

Begin in first position:

Kick the right leg forward, turned out, with the *toes pointed*, and let it swing down to the floor and back up behind you, then to the front and back down to first position. Repeat this forward, backward, front swing with the left leg. Keep both legs turned out. As the leg swings to the back, allow your torso to incline slightly forward. (Don't bend over, however.)

Repeat 8 to 16 times.

Try a slow count of 4 with a strong emphasis on the third kick.

LEVEL I
Circle stretch

This will help lengthen and slim your torso. Like a warm rubber band, you should now begin to feel what it is like to have skin, muscles, and sinew stretching for you. Enjoy it!

REMEMBER: Keep your weight evenly placed on both feet. Don't shift your weight as you bend sideways and down. As you circle upward, feel as though you were pulling off a wet T-shirt. Don't be afraid to pull and stretch as far away as possible.

For practice:
    4 times beginning to the left side; 4 times beginning to the right side. Repeat.

Begin in second position with arms overhead, fingers together.

    1. Keep the arms stretched as high as possible, feeling a pull through the torso.

    2. Bend at the waist to the left side.

    3. Continue circling down toward the floor. Keep both knees straight and the weight well over the balls of the feet, the

tummy pulled in, arms stretched. Continue this circular motion to the right, straightening up on the right side. Continue circling 4 times to the left and then reverse. Don't allow the hips to shift sideways; keep seat tight. 6 counts going down, 6 counts coming up.

LEVEL II
Sustained stretch

The amateur usually works too quickly and impetuously. The professional knows how to sustain effort. It takes time and patience to get the message from the brain to the parts of the body that you are addressing. See if you can sustain these positions until every part of your body is aware of what it is supposed to be feeling and doing.

REMEMBER: The goal is not to reach the floor but to control your movements; to know how to produce a real stretch, how to find and use your tummy muscles, to learn how to create suppleness without weakness in the back.

For practice:

Fingers together, turn your palms so they face the ceiling. Look up at your hands. Stay in this position until you have checked the accuracy of your stretch. Are your knees and *thighs* pulled up? Is your seat tight? Have you made your stomach disappear by pulling it in and up? Have you elongated your spine, visualizing each vertebra separated from every other vertebra? Have you dropped your shoulders so you don't mistake *that* feeling as the feeling of your spine being stretched? When you feel as though you have been compressed between two wooden slats, drop your head to your chest and slowly stretch the palms down to the floor in front of you. With all your strength pull your tummy up inside and create an arch out of the small of your back. Remain there for a few seconds. If you do not touch the floor, this is all right. Be sure to keep the weight over your toes, not on your heels. Check your seat. Did you let it move behind your heels? DON'T. Check your knees and thighs. Have you "pulled up" all the fat? *Slowly* raise back up. It takes a lot of mental—as well as physical—strength to control the impulse to speed up. Do not equate *faster* with *better*.

Repeat 8 to 16 times.

△ Breathing and Jumping

I have talked about breathing and its importance, but these principles must be put into practice. Don't underestimate the importance of these exercises, and don't be discouraged if you find them difficult in the beginning. Most people are very shallow breathers, i.e., they draw their breath from the surface rather than from deep inside. The lungs must be forced to use their full potential or capacity for air. These exercises will help develop that potential. As you practice, you will feel the pull of air move from your nose to deep inside your lungs, and you will begin to have the feeling that you have an infinite well of breath to draw upon. This increase of oxygen is the fuel for your eventual effortless exercising.

These exercises are part of a simple technique for building stamina. In the beginning, do not be alarmed if you see "black." Stop for a moment and put your head down, while sitting on the floor. This only means that you are getting more oxygen into your system than you are used to—which means you haven't been getting very much. You had better practice.

Rhythmical deep breathing is our key to stamina, but it must be practiced until it becomes second nature. Allow this rhythm to take over and do the work. Let the rhythm of breathing in and out become the wind to your sails. Without wind, how far or how smoothly would a sailboat move on a lake? Don't get out and push—let the principle of breathing go to work for you. That breath is your energy. There need be no shortage of that energy if you will cultivate it through use.

The simple fact is this: There should be a rhythm established between the exercise and the doing of it. In other words, it should not be haphazard. There should be orderly breathing and orderly exercising, and the two should be combined. When this happens, exercise gets smoother—and easier. You can work longer and with less fatigue. This is the secret of the stamina of the professional ballerina or athlete.

LEVEL I
Jumping in first
and second positions

Before you jump, establish the rhythm of your breathing. For 2 counts, breathe in smoothly through the nose. For 2 more counts, exhale that breath through your mouth. Don't be dainty about it. "Sniff" hard, exhale hard. Like a new balloon that in the beginning is hard to get started, those lungs have to be forced to expand. When you have established this pattern, add the jumps.

REMEMBER: Every jump must have a demi-plié at the beginning and end of it. The body must remain erect and not collapse in the middle. DON'T BE SURPRISED IF YOU CAN'T DO THIS TOO LONG IN THE BEGINNING. You are normal! But you'll know it's worth it when you can outlast all your friends on your next outing.

Take a slight rest between jumping combinations. Don't pause too long, however, because stamina is built up by smooth, consistent working habits. If the body is allowed to cool off, the muscles are working less efficiently.

For practice: Jumping in first position.

Jump 2 times in first position, using the inward breath. (Spread that breath evenly over the 2 jumps.) Continue 2 more jumps, exhaling that breath, and again smoothly forcing all the breath out. Repeat 16 times. As you build stamina, increase the number of jumps.

REMEMBER: The feet must land in a toe, ball, heel motion, *with the heels staying in contact with the floor once they land.* The knee must bend over the center of the foot. Keep the arms and shoulders relaxed. Don't raise the elbows as you jump.

For practice: Jumping to second position.
Repeat 8 times. Pause and repeat again.

1. Push heels down into the floor, bending the center of the knees over the middle of the feet. Keep the spine erect.

2. Spring up into the air, straightening the knees and pointing the toes.

3. Land with the feet apart in second position, bending the knees as soon as the heels touch the floor.

4. Immediately spring back up and return to first.

NOTE: If you are carrying around too much weight, lose some of it before you start jumping.

LEVEL II
Stamina builders

It is a wonderful feeling to get to the point where you enjoy moving, jumping, and running. There is a thrill when you *know* you have mastered your body and are telling *it* what to do. Believe me, it's worth the effort. At forty-two I thought I'd never jump again. At fifty I am jumping and running and dancing and having fun doing it!

Here are a few combinations to start with. The variations are of course endless.

REMEMBER: Always combine a breathing pattern with your jumping. It can vary according to your needs. That is, you can, if you wish, breathe in (and out) for a longer time, say for four jumps instead of two. As long as your breathing pattern is steady, rhythmical, and consistent, you are building toward easy and relaxed movement. *Be sure you always bend your knees when you land. Never, never come down on a straight leg.*

For practice:
Stand with feet parallel, arms relaxed, shoulders down:

1. Jump on the right foot 4 times, then on the left foot 4 times. Gradually increase the length of time you continue jumping.

Jump on the right foot 2 times, then on the left foot 2 times.

Jump on the right foot 1 time, then on the left foot 1 time.

Jump on the right foot 1 time, then on the left foot 1 time.

Repeat this combination several times, gradually increasing the number.

2. Begin in first position. Jump on both feet, lift the right foot behind the left ankle. Jump on both feet, lift the left foot behind right ankle.

Keep the arms slightly to the side. Don't allow them to move with the jumping.

Repeat 16 times. Pause and repeat.

3. Begin in third position. Jump with the feet apart to second position. (Keep the legs turned out, the knees turned sideways over the toes.) Jump back to the third position, putting the other foot in front this time.

Repeat 16 times. Pause and repeat.

△ *The Floor Work*

LEVEL I
The Butterfly

This sweeping movement lifts and strengthens the breast muscles while helping to relax the rigidity of the neck and shoulders.

REMEMBER: What you are feeling is important. Can you feel yourself a part of nature—with the freedom and grace of a butterfly? If not, why not?

To begin: Sit on floor, legs together, arms in front.

For practice:
8 times in all.

1. Bend forward pulling stomach in—reaching for toes. Tuck chin in. 3 counts.

2. Strongly sweep the arms and head upward. Continue the circle of the arms to the back. 3 counts.

3. Let the arms support the body as you lean backward, lifting the chest to ceiling. 3 counts.

4. Sweep arms back, up, and forward, stretching spine straight to begin again. 3 counts.

LEVEL II
Floor twist

I remember one day recently after I had skipped several days of exercising. My body felt brittle and rigid, as though it would break if I asked it to bend. The old panic of my early forties set in. Naturally that tightened me up even more. Then I got hold of myself and started reasoning with my head and heart. (*Don't forget, this is where the work must begin.*) I told my head that it was not logical to be afraid. I told my heart to get in touch with whatever emotions were causing so much tension. I conjured up images of warmth and softness. I gave myself permission to release, relax, and respond only to ease, softness, and pliability within—like a child. Then that image and those feelings reached my body, and it began to obey. Where before it was impossible to reach forward at all, my body began to soften and stretch again.

For practice:
Sitting on the floor with your legs together, open your arms sideways. Turn in your waist to the right side, turn your head to the right side, also. Bend forward,

stretching your left hand over your toes and lowering your left ear toward your knees. Keep stretching your right hand behind you. The arms should be creating a straight line front to back. Stretch forward twice and return to the upright position. Turn to the other side and repeat. Keep stretching your knees down to the floor and pointing your toes. Contract the stomach muscles each time. Don't hurry. Give yourself time to soften into the release of stretching.

Repeat 16 times.

LEVEL I
Sitting battements

This is a tummy strengthener. Each kick places a demand on the stomach muscles to contract and control the movement of the leg.

REMEMBER: Eventually you will be able to feel a big difference when you contract your abdomen. Don't give up because you don't experience this in the beginning.

For practice:
   Repeat 16 times, alternate legs after every 2 kicks.

   Lean back on your hands, chest lifted, back held straight. Contract and pull in the lower abdomen sharply.

   1. Lift the leg, keeping the inner abdominal muscles contracted. 2 counts.

   2. Lower the leg gently. 2 counts.

LEVEL II
Sitting battements—intermediate

Add the following three exercises only when you can do them without straining your back.

REMEMBER: Repeat these only as long as it is comfortable for you. Overdoing it makes no more sense for you than it does for a child. Our biggest fault is our impatience. Use your maturity to control this first!

For practice:

1. Lean back until you are resting on your elbows, your hands under your hips. Keep your legs straight ahead and turned out. Keep the torso facing straight ahead. If it turns toward the leg, you will not benefit from the stretch to the inside of the thighs. Kick one leg toward the side of the room, pointing your toes as hard as you can to the corner of the ceiling in a V effect. Be sure you allow the lower back to rest on the floor as you kick. Pull your stomach inside as this happens. Repeat with the other leg.

Repeat 16 times.

2. In the same leaning back position, this time with the legs turned straight, kick over your head, adding a second kick while it is still back there. (Try to get it back a little farther.) The toes are pointed as you kick it back. The foot flexes as you make the second thrust. The head comes forward toward your knee, the stomach contracts. Then lower the leg. Repeat with the other leg.

Give two counts to each backward thrust, two counts as you lower the leg to the floor.

Repeat 16 times.

3. This should be attempted only if you are in good condition. Rest on your elbows, hands under your hips, legs turned out. Raise one leg. Change the legs in the air four times. 4 counts. Then raise the leg from the floor so that you are holding both legs together over your stomach. (Point your feet as much as you can.) Hold for 3 counts, then lower one leg to the floor on the fourth count, and start over. As the legs are held together in the air pull your stomach down into the floor for the three counts. Keep the knees straight, the feet pointed.

Be sure you lower the base of the spine to the floor so there is no undue pressure on it. This is accomplished by allowing the lower back to "rest" on the floor.

Try to establish a breathing pattern so you are not holding your breath.

Repeat 4 to 8 times.

LEVEL I
Roll-ups

This exercise is wonderful for strengthening the lower spine. I can't tell you the number of women who have come to me with back problems, most of them due to the incredible lack of flexibility and improper use of the lower spine when exercising and to incorrect posture habits. These same women later exclaim how they no longer suffer. All they needed was the oiling and flexing that keeps the spine healthy and pain free, along with the knowledge about correct alignment of their spines. No single exercise will cure your back problems, but all of these exercises together are going to help. This one in particular is gentle and beneficial for the majority of women. You must not approach this exercise as if it were a masculine, tough bit of gym work. Conventional "sit-ups" may do something positive for the male body but very little for the female who invariably strains upward. Rolling up is your protection.

REMEMBER: You must come up smoothly, and slowly! Use your arms and elbows on the floor to help yourself roll down and up, one vertebra at a time. It is the gentle unwinding that "oils" the spine. The goal is to control each vertebra in a rolling motion. It is NOT to see how much strength you can exhibit by jerking upright.

For practice:

Bend your knees, placing the feet on the floor where it feels comfortable to you. Slowly roll down your spine, little by little, until you reach the floor. Roll up. Repeat 8 times, adding more only as you get stronger.

1. Drop your chin on your chest, contract your abdominal muscles, "curl" your body, and begin to go back.

2. Allow your knees to move slightly backward with you until you can feel the lowest vertebrae touching the floor first. Keep your knees together, your chin on your chest, your stomach pulled inside.

3. When you reach the floor allow the legs to straighten and let the breath out of your body. Pause a few seconds, and begin to come back up by bringing your chin forward, bending your knees, and

allowing your elbows and arms to position themselves where they support your body weight while you "curl" back up to the starting position. 12 counts down, 12 counts up.

LEVEL II
Roll-ups—advanced

If you are quite sure you are lowering one vertebra at a time onto the floor, beginning with the tailbone and proceeding from there, then you may try this. Don't rush into this however. Always keep in mind that achieving correct technique is what is important and will lead to real improvement.

REMEMBER: All exercise should be a fifty / fifty balance of effort *and* relaxation. You are in training to achieve that balance. See if you can tell what your percentages are.

For practice:
With your legs together and your knees straight, reach forward and hold on to your ankles. Drop your head, contract your stomach muscles, and begin to *roll* the spine back onto the floor. As you curve and lower the spine, it will pull your legs back a little with it. This is correct. Keep the knees straight, the toes pointed. As the head goes onto the floor, move your arms over your head to the back. Release the breath and feel the body

"deflate." Bring the arms and chin forward. *Slowly* and *evenly* roll up, again one vertebra at a time. Press the small of the back into the floor as you begin coming up. Keep the shoulders and arms soft and relaxed. Don't jerk up. Don't push up. Don't strain up. Control this with your stomach muscles, leaving your shoulders and arms out of it. Finally, reach forward again, holding on to your ankles, and bend your head to your knees, chin on your chest. Pull the stomach in.

Repeat 8 times; 12 counts rolling down, 12 counts curling up.

LEVEL I
The arch or cat stretch

There is nothing like this wonderful stretch on the floor to make you feel your whole body is involved in extending itself beyond its limits. You must allow yourself to feel as though you were lying in the sun stretching, with the warm, lazy, uninhibited movement of a cat.

REMEMBER: The body responds to one's visual image. See yourself elongated and narrow, like pulling out warm taffy, and your body will yield and gradually correspond to this visualization.

For practice:
  Slowly turn to alternate sides. 8 times in all.

  1. Lie on your back, arms stretched over your head. Allow one knee to bend slightly with the foot on the floor. Let your stomach "sink" into the floor. Push yourself gently onto your side, straightening both knees and pointing your toes. Keep the seat very tight.

  2. Slightly arch your entire body, pushing your legs and arms a little way behind

you to form an elongated crescent. Look up at your hands. Feel the length of the body yield and stretch in both directions. You should experience a pull and flattening of the entire stomach and chest. The first time or two test that "flatness" by putting one hand on your stomach. Return hand above and roll gently onto your back. Raise the other knee slightly and push to the other side. 12 counts for each side.

LEVEL II
Relaxation technique

Do you know how to get rid of tension in every part of your body? Here is a routine that—with practice—should help you identify and dissolve that pressure within.

REMEMBER: Follow these steps in sequence. Move slowly and calmly. You must be willing to give up your resistance.

To begin: lie on the floor—arms comfortably to the side.

1. Close your eyes.

2. Inhale deeply, exhale slowly.

3. Allow yourself to visualize the following picture. You are floating on a lake or lying on a water mattress. It is a warm, quiet, lazy day for you.

4. Wiggle your toes. Lift one leg a little way off the floor. As if it were too heavy, drop it gently. Repeat with the other foot and leg. Feel as though your hips widen, open, and relax.

5. Make a little sigh.

6. Wiggle your fingers. Raise one arm. Let it go limp and fall "into the water." Repeat with the other arm.

7. Picture your body as a balloon that you now fill with air by taking a long, big breath. As you slowly exhale feel the balloon deflate, relaxing everything inside you—stomach, chest, muscles.

8. Take your fingers and gently "pin" your shoulders into the floor making your chest and back as wide as possible. Drop the backs of your hands "in the water."

9. Raise your head one inch. Allow it to drop deeply into the mattress with a big sigh—"seeing" all the pressure in your body floating away from you with the ripples in the water.

10. Allow the neck and the back of your head to soften and rest.

11. Open your mouth, drop your jaw moving it lazily to each side. Move the tongue and let it hang loosely inside your mouth with the lips gently parted.

12. Smooth your forehead—gently stretching the eyebrows.

13. Gently close your eyes, "seeing" only light blue space that fills your entire head.

14. "Hear" the sound of the water as you "float."

15. Breathe gently, simply, rhythmically. *Feel* the peace.

16. Memorize this feeling of ease—and when any intruding feeling occurs, recognize it and train yourself to eliminate it.

LEVEL I
Floor battements

With the floor supporting you, you have the opportunity for a stronger thrust of the leg while keeping your back straight. The idea is to feel this stretch from your toes up to your ribcage as though your leg and its movement began there. When practiced carefully, this is a wonderful exercise to reduce the outside of your thighs and firm the seat. Then you should repeat it straight up to reach the inside of the thighs.

REMEMBER: The body must be as carefully in alignment on the floor as it is when you are standing. The exercise will not work for you if you allow your seat to fall behind you. You must visualize both the front and back of you as "flattened" between two opposing forces or walls, and keep it that way as you kick.

For practice:
    Repeat 16 times to the back. After that, repeat 16 times straight up. Turn and repeat with the other leg.
    Placing a little weight forward on your hand in front of your chest, kick the leg to

the back. As you do so, pinch the seat together both outside and between your legs as tightly as you can. The leg will not be far back, or high. DO NOT LET THE SEAT SEPARATE OR THE STOMACH PUSH OUTWARD. Keep the knees stretched, the toes pointed as you kick back each time. If you allow the buttocks to "soften," it will not benefit you. 2 counts to lift leg, 2 counts to return it.

NOTE: When kicking sideways, the goal is to stretch the inside of the thighs. This can only happen when your seat remains tightly together. Turn the leg out as you kick. As when you are standing, kicking the leg "high" must not take priority over kicking correctly.

LEVEL II
Exercising the artist

Now, while I sit in the corner to encourage you, it is *your* turn to exercise your creative muscles, to release your feelings, to stretch the limits of your imagination.

You have prepared your body, the canvas for the expression of your soul—the frame that contains the creation of your mood, your hue or color, your concrete or abstract expression. What will it be? Who are you deep down inside? You may never know until you begin to bring her to the surface.

Play music that arouses your spirit. Begin to move freely and spontaneously to it. Close out the intruders called timidity, hesitancy, self-consciousness. Dare to indulge—and enjoy—you, and know that that enjoyment is proper and correct, for it is the deeper, fuller, richer you that now deserves expression. Turn, sway, bend, reach, skip, run—create your own ballet movement and make it fun!

Index

Face, 49-51
    exercise for, 50
Feelings, 77-78
Feet, 45-48
    exercise for, 47
    positions of, *See* First position; Second position; Third
        position; Parallel
Fifth position, 101-2
First position, 82, 86-88
    jumping in, 173-75
Fitzgerald, Zelda, 64
Flexed battements, 160-61
Floor battements, 199-200
Floor twist, 182-83
Floor work, 179-201
    arch (cat stretch), 194-95
    butterfly, 179-81
    definition of, 82
    exercising the artist, 201
    relaxation technique, 196-98
    roll-ups, 189-91
    roll-ups, advanced, 192-93
    sitting battements, 184-85
    sitting battements, intermediate, 186-88
Food, 59-61
Forward port de bras, 119-23
    en relevé, 122-23
Forward stretch and arch, 143-47

Goethe, Johann Wolfgang, 25
Grands battements, 113-18
    en croix, 117-18
Grands pliés, 95-97
    in third position, 102-3